DELICIOUSLY VEGAN,

DELICIOUSLY GLUTEN FREE

*Mouth-watering, plant-based recipes
for the gluten intolerant*

By

Michelle Berriedale-Johnson

CONTENTS

IIIIIIIIIIIIIIIIIIIIIIIIIIIIIIIIIII

INTRODUCTION

|||||||||||||||||||||||||||||||||

I have been creating free-from recipes for over 30 years, first for our allergy magazine, then for over a dozen free-from books. I founded the FreeFrom Food Awards in 2008 and they are still the UK's only free-from award for food and drink. I also run the FoodsMatter website, a resource for food allergy and intolerance, so I have come up with a good few free-from food recipes during my career.

Some of the recipes in this book are created by Katherine Winter, an excellent free-from cook and chef at the FreeFrom Food Awards judging sessions. She has two children and a hungry and discerning husband, so her recipes have also been tested at the coal face. She is a much better dessert and baking cook than I am so you will find that a number of the dessert and baking recipes have her signature.

You will also find a handful of recipes from the 'Simply Italian, Simply Gluten Free' book that I published last year with the wonderful Italian cook, Anna Del Conte. For those of you who do not know her, Anna, who is now heading towards her 96th birthday, is a deep well of knowledge about everything to do with traditional, historical, and regional Italian food and cooking. It took me a long time to persuade her that gluten-free pasta might not taste the same as durum wheat pasta but that it did still taste good, and that gluten-free, traditional Italian dishes would work. As it turns out, many of her more classic dishes use olive oil rather than butter and really do not need the addition of cheese — so were already vegan!

I believe that cooking should be an adventure and that, as with most things in life, the only way you learn to get it right is by getting it wrong first. So, while my recipes do tell you what to do, they also encourage you to experiment and above all to taste — to taste for flavour, to taste for texture, and to adapt what you are doing accordingly. By tasting continually, you will learn how to develop recipes to suit your own palate, but just as exciting, learn to enjoy other combinations of flavours and textures which you might never have thought of. So be adventurous. The more often you try, the more often you are likely to get it right!

Happy cooking...

BREAKFAST

||||||||||||||||||||||||||||||

Hash browns

Mushrooms and tofu with za'atar

Vegan Spanish 'omelette'

Gluten-free granola

Beetroot, kale, and walnut smoothie

Pea, banana, and chia seed smoothie

Although I am quite set in my breakfast ways, the occasional splurge on something new — or an exciting dish for that weekend brunch — is always tempting. So, I have added a couple of brunch dishes for a sunny Sunday morning.

There are also a few smoothie ideas from my good friend Sonja in the West of Ireland. She has shared her recipes but says that these are only ideas, and you should feel free to add (or remove) ingredients and make the smoothie thicker or thinner according to yours, and your family's taste.

She also makes delicious granola.

HASH BROWNS

Perfect Sunday morning breakfast with some vegan bacon — or just on their own. The starchy aquafaba helps to hold the potato together to form a relatively solid patty.

INGREDIENTS
SERVES 4

700g /1 ½ lbs floury old or baking potatoes

1 large onion

100ml/3fl oz/scant ½ cup aquafaba or liquid from a can of chickpeas

sea salt and freshly ground black pepper

1–2 tbsp sunflower or rapeseed oil for frying

METHOD

Peel and grate the potatoes and the onion coarsely.

Put both into a clean tea towel and squeeze thoroughly to get out as much liquid as possible.

Put in a bowl, add the aquafaba and season generously. Mix thoroughly.

Just cover the bottom of a wide non-stick pan with oil, and heat.

Take a tablespoon of the potato mixture and place it in the pan, then flatten it out into a patty no more than 2cm/1 inch thick, with a wooden spoon or a spatula.

Fry for 3–5 minutes (depending on how thick your patty is) on either side or till nicely browned and crisp.

Serve at once.

MUSHROOMS AND TOFU WITH ZA'ATAR

A delicious brunch dish. Combining the soy sauce with the za'atar seems a slightly odd mixture of culinary cultures, but it works so well that I hope purists will forgive me.

INGREDIENTS
SERVES 4

4 tbsp coconut oil + 2 tbsp olive oil

6 cloves garlic, peeled and sliced finely

200g/8 oz plain tofu, cut into small cubes

300g/12 oz mushrooms — portobello, chestnut or button, sliced or chopped roughly

2 tbsp gluten-free soy sauce

sea salt and freshly ground black pepper

4 slices wholemeal gluten-free bread

extra coconut oil for the toast

4 level tsp za'atar

METHOD

Heat 3 tablespoons of the coconut oil in a wide pan and add the garlic.

Gently cook the garlic for a couple of minutes, then add the tofu and continue to fry — taking care not to burn the garlic — until the tofu turns very gently golden. This will take about 5 minutes.

Add the extra coconut oil and the olive oil and then the mushrooms.

Cook fairly briskly for another 3–4 minutes or until the mushrooms have given their juices

Add the soy sauce and then season to taste.

Meanwhile, toast the bread and spread with some coconut oil.

Pile the mushroom mixture on the toast, sprinkle each serving with a teaspoon of za'atar and serve at once.

VEGAN SPANISH 'OMELETTE'

This is seriously tasty, although the aquafaba and gram flour do not really replicate the texture of eggs as they do not hold the vegetables together in the way that eggs would. But the result is nonetheless delicious — and perfect for a reviving brunch after a morning run.

INGREDIENTS
SERVES 4

4 tbs sunflower or coconut oil

1 large or 2 medium onions, peeled and sliced thinly

2 large cloves garlic, peeled and sliced thinly

1 large stick celery, chopped small

1 small hot chilli, deseeded and cut into thin batons

1 medium red bell pepper, deseeded and sliced thinly

4 large mushrooms, sliced

10 small plum tomatoes, halved crossways

150g/6 oz cooked potatoes, cut into small dice

sea salt and freshly ground black pepper

250ml/8fl oz/1 cup aquafaba (the liquid from a can of chickpeas). You may need to open two cans of chickpeas to get that much aquafaba — so be ready to make some hummus.

40g/1 ½ oz chickpea/gram flour

75g/3 oz strong vegan cheddar, grated

a large handful of flat-leaf parsley, chopped fairly small

METHOD

Heat the oil in a large, wide pan and add the onions, garlic, celery, chilli, red pepper, and a pinch of salt.

Fry fairly gently, making sure not to burn, for 5–10 minutes or until the vegetables are starting to soften.

Add the mushrooms and the tomatoes and continue to fry gently for a further 5-10 minutes or until all the vegetables are cooked.

Add the potatoes stir well in and season to taste.

Whisk the aquafaba in a bowl till light and fluffy and then stir in the gram flour, grated cheese and chopped parsley. Mix well.

Pour into the vegetables and mix well. Be aware that it will tend to 'fluff' over the edges of your pan, so you need to treat it with care.

Continue to cook over a low heat, stirring periodically to distribute the aquafaba mix, for approximately 10 minutes.

Remove from the heat and serve with a large spoon.

GLUTEN-FREE GRANOLA

I have used gluten-free porridge oats but if you don't want to use oats you could also make the granola with buckwheat or rice, quinoa, or millet flakes, although you might need to up the honey content slightly to counteract the bitterness of quinoa and millet flakes.

I prefer to put fresh fruit on top of my granola rather than dried fruit in it, but if you like to include dried fruit, then do so at the end once it has cooked.

If you are using dried fruit, try to make sure it is not too dried and hard. Don't soak it as that will make it wet and spoil the crunchy texture of your granola.

This makes 4–6 servings depending on how generous you are with your servings. To make a big batch for storage just double up on the quantities and spread it over several baking trays to cook.

INGREDIENTS

200g/8 oz gluten free porridge oats, or buckwheat, or rice, millet, or quinoa flakes

pinch salt or less

75g/3 oz flax seeds or chia seeds or a mixture of the two

50g/2oz/ each sunflower and pumpkin seeds

100g/4oz/¾ cup broken nuts of your choice – my favourites are hazelnuts, walnuts, almonds and cashews but feel free to use your own favourites

1 tbsp coconut oil

1 tbsp either honey or maple syrup

1 tbsp each of 2 or 3 dried fruits of your choice. If you are using large fruit such as apricots or prunes, you might want to cut them in half or quarters. Fruit optional.

METHOD

In large bowl combine the oats/flakes, seeds, and nuts. Melt the oil and honey or maple syrup together and then mix thoroughly into dry ingredients.

Spread mix on a baking tray and bake at 160°C for 40 minutes, stirring every 10 minutes to ensure even baking. Remove when golden. Cool.

Mix in dried fruit if you are using it. Store in airtight containers.

BEETROOT, KALE AND WALNUT SMOOTHIE

INGREDIENTS
SERVES 1-2

1 medium sized raw beetroot, trimmed and scrubbed

large handful of kale (stems removed) well washed

1-2 thick slices ginger root, depending how keen you are on ginger. You don't need to peel it

1 stick celery (optional)

a handful of broken walnuts

½ a lemon

an apple (unpeeled) or an orange (peeled)

300-450ml/10-15fl oz/1-1 ½ cups water (or fruit juice) depending on how thick or thin you like your smoothie

METHOD
Put all ingredients into a smoothie maker, liquidizer, or food processor and, starting slowly, whizz until it is as 'bitty' or 'smooth' as you like it.

PEA, BANANA AND CHIA SEED SMOOTHIE

INGREDIENTS
SERVES 1-2

1 tbsp chia seeds

300ml/10fl oz/1 ¼ cups almond milk — either a proprietary one or your own made from 2 tbsp of almond butter whizzed with 300ml/10fl oz/1 ¼ cups water

Generous tsp of sea salad mix, or dried seaweed (you might want to soak this for 10-15 minutes in a little hot water to soften it)

100g/4 oz frozen peas

1 frozen sliced banana

METHOD

Soak the chia seeds in the almond milk for 30 minutes before making the smoothie.

If you are using dried seaweed rather than sea salad, soak it in boiling water for 30 minutes, then drain and chop.

Put all the ingredients into your smoothie maker, liquidiser or food processor and blend slowly to start and then blitz until smooth.

SOUPS

Any root veg soup

Corn chowder

Parsnip and ginger

Leek top soup

Anna's pea and pear soup

Moroccan carrot and red lentil soup

Green pea and wasabi soup

Chilled borscht with apple

Wholemeal rice soup

Grated carrot and onion soup

I love soup. If you are cold, it warms you, if you are hungry, it fills you, if you are sad, it comforts you, if you are too hot it can cool you, if you don't feel well, it is easy to eat — and it is so easy to make. I rarely use a recipe now, allowing what I find in the shop or the market to guide each day's combination. Sometimes

I grate the vegetables, sometimes I purée them; sometimes I add rice, or lentils or pasta, sometimes I add fruits and herbs; sometimes I combine lots of ingredients; sometimes I stick to one or two; sometimes I sprinkle nuts or seeds on top before serving, sometimes I spice it up with some harissa or chilli flakes, sometimes I just swirl in some plant-based yogurt or vegan cream.

So do use the following recipes as guidance, but actually, let your soup genie lead you. It is very hard to make a bad soup so be brave and experiment — you won't regret it.

ANY ROOT VEG SOUP

Making a delicious root vegetable soup is so simple, so warming, so nourishing and so filling that, in winter at least, it should be on everyone's menu every week. Even in summer, root vegetable soups can be delicious chilled and generously sprinkled with chopped fresh parsley, coriander, or edible flowers.

I could give you weights and measures but that slows the whole process down, so I suggest that you fly free. This will have the virtue that every batch will be slightly different as your quantities and ingredients change.

INGREDIENTS
SERVES 4

1 fairly large saucepan

you can use a single vegetable or a combination but probably keep it to a maximum of three otherwise the flavours get rather muddled. My favourites are parsnips, sweet potatoes, celeriac, butternut squash and carrots. I sometimes add beetroot, but it does tend to take the soup over

root vegetables of your choice – you need enough to $^2/_3 - ^3/_4$ fill your saucepan when they are chopped up. I scrub my vegetables and only peel them if the skins are very coarse – some sweet potatoes for example – and cut them into large pieces

you can also use a small amount potato but unless you use very floury potatoes, they can give a rather glutinous texture to the soup

onions. I sometimes add an onion or a leek – peeled and sliced thickly – but this is not necessary

approx. 1 litre/2 pints/4 ¼ cups soya, oat, nut, coconut, or whatever plant-based milk you like

approx. 500ml/18fl oz/2 cups gluten and wheat free vegetable stock or gluten free miso

salt and freshly ground black pepper

METHOD

Add the liquid to the vegetables in the saucepan, bring slowly to the boil then simmer, covered for 20–40 minutes (depending on the vegetable) until the vegetables are soft.

Remove from the heat and purée in a liquidiser or food processor. Season to taste and, if it is too thick, add more stock or miso and readjust the seasoning.

Serve on its own, sprinkled with toasted seeds, pine nuts, chilli flakes or fresh herbs or with a swirl of coconut or soya yogurt or cream and lots of freshly ground black pepper.

CORN CHOWDER

A warming and filling winter soup. The chilli is not traditional in a chowder but does give the soup a bit of an extra dimension.

INGREDIENTS
SERVES 4

1 tbsp coconut or olive oil

1 medium onion, peeled and finely chopped

½-1 small red chilli, depending on how hot a kick you want your chowder to have

1 large stick celery, chopped small

1 small yellow pepper, deseeded and cut in small pieces

200g/8 oz white potato, scrubbed and cut into small (10cm/½ inch) pieces

200g/8 oz sweetcorn, fresh, frozen, or canned (drained)

3 bay leaves

500ml/16fl oz/2 cups hazelnut milk — or if you cannot eat nuts, soya, or coconut milk

300ml/10fl oz/ 1¼ cup gluten and gluten and wheat free vegetable stock

sea salt and freshly ground black pepper

2 slices of vegan bacon, crumbled (optional)

METHOD

Heat the oil in a deep pan and add the onion, chilli, celery and pepper and sauté gently for 15–20 minutes or until the vegetables are softening.

Add the potato dice, sweetcorn, and bay leaves with which ever milk you are using and the stock.

Bring to the boil, cover, and simmer for 45 minutes.

Season to taste and serve sprinkled with the crumbled vegan bacon if you are using it.

PARSNIP AND GINGER SOUP

Parsnip and ginger are a great combination, but you need to decide before you start how gingery you want it to be. About 15g/½ oz will give a gentle flavour of ginger permeating the soup; 25g/1 oz will give a serious ginger kick.

You can use whichever non-dairy milk you like or are able to tolerate. Obviously, the milk you use will slightly affect the flavour of the soup — but the ginger and the parsnip together are powerful enough to hold their own.

INGREDIENTS
SERVES 4

2 large parsnips, scrubbed, topped, tailed, and sliced thickly

15–25g/½ – 1 oz fresh ginger root, trimmed of any rough bits and chopped

600ml/1 ¼ pints/2 ½ cups oat, coconut, nut, or soya milk

600ml/1 ¼ pints/2 ½ cups gluten-free vegetable stock

sea salt and freshly ground black pepper

4 heaped tsp plain coconut yogurt

50g/2oz toasted pine nuts (optional)

METHOD

Put the sliced parsnips with the ginger in a large pan with whichever milk you are using and the vegetable stock.

Bring to the boil and simmer, covered, for 20–25 minutes or until the parsnips are very soft.

Purée in a food processor or liquidiser.

Season to taste and, if the soup is too thick, thin with vegetable stock or plant-based milk.

Reheat to serve with a teaspoon of plain coconut yoghurt swirling into each bowl or sprinkled with toasted pine nuts — or both.

LEEK TOP SOUP

If you get your leeks from a veg box or a farm shop rather than pre-packed from a supermarket, they will come with a huge sheaf of green tops. Most people cut these off and either throw them out or add them to the compost. But why? They make excellent stock and actually, a rather delicate soup.

If you want to add a bit of kick, sprinkle the soup with some finely crushed chilli flakes.

INGREDIENTS
SERVES 4

6 large leeks with lots of green tops

1 litre/2 pints/4 ¼ cups water or a mild gluten free vegetable stock

250ml/9fl oz/1 cup dryish white wine

sea salt and freshly ground black pepper

dried chilli flakes (optional)

METHOD

Cut off the green parts of the leeks, reserve the whites for another dish and wash the green leaves thoroughly — earth often gets wedged down between them.

Put the leeks in a large pan with the water or stock and the white wine. Bring to the boil and simmer gently, covered, for an hour.

For the stock: drain the leeks from the liquid (and compost them) and reserve the liquid for use in another dish.

For the soup: purée the leeks and their liquid thoroughly in a liquidiser or food processer and return to the pan.

Season to taste and if the soup is too thick, thin with gluten-free vegetable stock.

Reheat and serve alone or with a dusting of crushed red chilli flakes.

ANNA'S PEA AND PEAR SOUP

I have a great weakness for fruit soups. They do not need to be sweet, but the addition of a little fruit can give a delicious edge to the vegetables. This recipe is one from the lovely Italian cook Anna del Conte and appears in her 'Simply Italian, Simply Gluten Free' cookbook that we published last year. Anna's original recipe included butter and cream, but I persuaded her that the soup worked even better without the dairy products which just masked the flavours of the peas, the pears, and the mint.

INGREDIENTS
SERVES 4

1 onion, very finely sliced

4 tbsp olive oil

sea salt

12 mint leaves, torn

2 ripe pears, peeled and cut into small pieces

500g/1 lb frozen petits pois

1 litre/2 pints/4 ¼ cups gluten free vegetable stock

freshly ground black pepper

METHOD

Gently sauté the onion, together with a pinch of salt and half the torn mint leaves in the oil for 8–10 minutes, stirring frequently. The onion should become soft and golden brown.

Add the pear to the onion. Sauté for 1 minute then add the petits pois with all their ice attached. Mix well and then add the stock.

Bring to the boil and simmer for 10 minutes.

Blend the soup with a stick blender or in a liquidiser or food processor and season to taste.

Sprinkle a little mint over each bowl before serving.

MOROCCAN CARROT AND RED LENTIL SOUP

Lovely spicy soup — just given an edge by the lemon juice. Be sure to check the harissa ingredients if you buy it readymade — or you could make your own.

INGREDIENTS
SERVES 4

2 tbsp olive oil

3 large cloves garlic peeled and sliced

2 level tsp ground cumin

½ level tsp ground coriander

275g/11 oz carrots, scrubbed and sliced

200g/8 oz red lentils

1 litre/2 pints/4 ¼ cups gluten/wheat-free vegetable stock

sea salt and freshly ground black pepper

juice 1–2 lemons

harissa spice mix or harissa paste — check ingredients for gluten and allergens

METHOD

Heat the oil in a heavy pan and add the garlic, cumin, and coriander. Stir and cook for a minute or two taking great care that it does not burn.

Add the carrots and continue to cook gently for a further 5 minutes.

Add the lentils and the stock, bring to the boil, cover, and simmer for 35–40 minutes or until the carrots are quite cooked.

Purée in a processor or liquidiser and adjust the seasoning to taste. If the soup is too thick, thin with a little extra stock.

To serve, reheat, check the seasoning, and add lemon juice to taste.

Sprinkle a pinch of harissa over each bowl as you serve it – or swirl ¼–½ teaspoonful of harissa paste into each bowl, depending on how spicy you want your soup to taste.

GREEN PEA AND WASABI SOUP

A very simple soup but rather delicate in flavour — the wasabi comes through just as you have stopped expecting it to! And it is a fabulous colour.

INGREDIENTS
SERVES 4

700g/1 lb 5 oz of frozen petits pois

1 large leek, sliced thickly

500ml/18fl oz/2 cups plain soya, oat, coconut, or almond milk

500ml/18fl oz/2 cups gluten and wheat free vegetable stock

3 tsp wasabi powder – level or heaped, depending on how strong you would like the wasabi kick to be

sea salt and freshly ground black pepper

METHOD

Put the petits pois and leek in a pan with whatever milk you are using. Add the stock and bring to the boil.

Simmer gently for 5 minutes then purée in a food processor.

Pass the soup through a coarse sieve — this is quite hard work but worth it if you want a smooth soup.

Mix the wasabi powder into a paste with a little water, then add a teaspoonful at a time to the soup. Mix till smooth.

Transfer back to the main bowl and season to taste if you need to.

Serve either hot or chilled but if you serve it chilled you may need to thin it with a little extra milk or stock.

CHILLED BORSCHT WITH APPLE

Bortsch is normally served hot but this chilled version is a wonderful colour and really refreshing on a hot day. The apple gives it an interesting extra dimension.

INGREDIENTS
SERVES 4

350g/14 oz raw beetroots/beets, topped, tailed, and scrubbed

150g /6 oz sweet potato, peeled

1 small Bramley or other sharp cooking apple, cored but not peeled

1 litre/2 pints/4 ¼ cups gluten and wheat-free vegetable stock

sea salt and freshly ground black pepper

4 tbsp soya or coconut yogurt

METHOD

Halve or quarter the beetroot and put in a large pan with the sweet potato, apple, and stock.

Bring to the boil, cover, and simmer gently for 45–60 minutes or until the beets are quite cooked.

Purée in a food processor then return to the pan.

Adjust seasoning to taste then chill.

Check the seasoning as chilling can dull the flavour.

To serve pour into a tureen or individual bowls and swirl the yogurt into the middle of each bowl.

WHOLEMEAL RICE SOUP

For barley lovers who can no longer eat barley, this soup will be a revelation. Cook the rice long and slowly enough and it will taste just like barley! Super simple — a lovely winter soup.

INGREDIENTS
SERVES 4

4 tbsp olive oil

2 large leeks, finely sliced

100g/4 oz wholegrain rice

1.8 litres/4 pints/7 ½ cups vegetable stock

sea salt and freshly ground black pepper

DELICIOUSLY VEGAN, DELICIOUSLY GLUTEN FREE

METHOD

Heat the oil in a deep pan and add the leeks.

Reduce the heat very low, cover and sweat the leeks for at least 15 minutes.

Add the rice, stir around so that the grains get coated with the oil, then add the stock.

Bring slowly to the boil, reduce to a simmer, cover, and cook very gently for 2 – 3 hours.

The rice will gradually release all of its starch, and the soup with become thick and luscious.

Season to taste and thin with extra stock if it is too thick.

GRATED CARROT AND ONION SOUP

The trick to this soup is to cook the carrots and onions long and slow before you add the stock. Don't rush it as the flavour will definitely suffer. This treatment will also work really well with any hard root vegetable such as parsnips, celeriac, turnips or beetroot; it doesn't work with softer roots such as sweet potatoes or squash which are better puréed.

INGREDIENTS
SERVES 4 GENEROUSLY

4 large onions – approx. 700g/1 lb 12 oz

4 large carrots – approx. 500g/1 lb 4 oz

100g/2 heaped tbsp coconut oil

1 litre 500ml/2 ½ pints/6 $^1/_3$ cups gluten free vegetable stock or gluten free miso

sea salt and freshly ground black pepper

METHOD

Peel and slice the onions thinly.

Scrub the carrots and grate coarsely.

Melt the oil in a heavy pan and add the onions and carrots.

Cook very gently, uncovered and stirring regularly to make sure they don't burn, for at least 25-30 minutes. The longer the better

Add the stock, bring to the boil and simmer for anther 30 minutes.

Season to taste.

DIPS

||||||||||||||||||||||||||||

Hummus variations

Butter bean/lima bean hummus

Avocado and cannellini bean dip with pine nuts

Ajwar

Aubergine/eggplant and nut butter pâté

HUMMUS AND VARIATIONS

Just a few suggestions, mainly pulse based for dips as they are so useful. In sandwiches, in wraps, on a salad, with crudités, with gluten-free toast, in a lunchbox. Tasty, easy, and healthy.

Hummus has really become *THE* go to snack. While the original chickpea version is still my favourite, it is very easy to create an almost infinite range of alternatives. So below is my classic hummus recipe with a series of suggestions for additions.

Some people also find homemade hummus too rich and solid; adding a couple of handfuls of crushed ice can lighten the texture.

If I am making hummus for a party, I always use dried chickpeas as I prefer both the flavour and texture (both slightly nuttier). However, using dried chickpeas is quite a performance as the chickpeas need to be soaked and then cooked. As long as you soak your chickpeas overnight, it is relatively easy but if I am only making a small amount, I use canned.

FOR A BIG PARTY

If I am making for a party, I make lots as it will keep in the fridge for a week to 10 days and, if you really have too much, you can always freeze it. So, I would use 250g – 500g/9 oz – 1 lb 2 oz dried chickpeas and then add then ingredients below until I am happy with the taste and texture.

You will need to soak the dried chickpeas in plenty of cold water overnight. Then drain them and put them in a large pan well covered with more water. Bring to the boil and simmer for 3 – 4 hours, topping up the water as needed. You want them to be soft but not mushy.

INGREDIENTS
FOR A SMALLER GROUP OF 4 - 6.

2 x 400g/14 oz cans chickpeas, drained but not very well so some of the liquid remains

3–5 cloves garlic, peeled and sliced

approx 150ml/5fl oz/ 2/3 cup extra virgin olive oil

2 tbsp tahini (traditional but optional)

2–3 lemons

sea salt and freshly ground black pepper

2 handfuls of crushed ice (optional)

METHOD

Put the chickpeas and their remaining liquid in a food processor with 2 of the garlic cloves, 100ml/3fl oz/$^1/_3$ cup of the oil, the tahini, and the juice of 1 $^1/_2$ lemons. If you like your hummus more garlicky, add more cloves.

Whizz until quite smooth.

Continue to add garlic, olive oil, lemon juice, sea salt and black pepper until you are happy with the flavour and the texture.

If you want the texture to be lighter, add the crushed ice, bit by bit until you achieve the texture you want.

Serve with raw vegetables or gluten-free toast.

VARIATIONS:

Instead of the tahini, add any of the following to the mixture. You may want to reduce the amount of garlic that you use, and in some combinations, you may want to leave out the lemon juice, but feel free to experiment with other additions — just be sure to taste and season as you go.

- 1 ripe avocado plus chilli flakes or harissa to taste — lemon juice optional

- large handful of pitted black olives and a generous handful of fresh coriander/cilantro

- passata (thick, concentrated tomato purée) or tomato purée, a handful of pitted black olives and chilli flakes – lemon juice optional

- handful of seaweed salad

- handfuls of baby leaf spinach, fresh parsley, spring onions/ scallions, chives, or coriander/cilantro

- a couple of small, cooked beets/beetroots

- fresh horseradish root or horseradish sauce (be sure to check the ingredients)

- sliced red bell pepper that has been cooked long and slowly in oil; or red peppers bottled or tinned in oil; or the flesh of red peppers that have been grilled/broiled to burn off their skins – plus harissa to taste

BUTTER BEAN/LIMA BEAN HUMMUS

Much as I love chickpeas, I also love butter beans, so I just wondered how hummus would work with a different pulse. Actually, very well...

INGREDIENTS
SERVES 4 - 6

2 x 400g /14 oz cans butter beans, drained

2 large cloves garlic, crushed

2 small bird's eye green peppers, deseeded and chopped small

100ml /3fl oz/ 1/3 cup coconut milk

sea salt and freshly ground black pepper

METHOD
Put all the ingredients except the seasoning into a food processor and whiz, then season to taste.

Serve with raw or blanched vegetables (I use yellow peppers and very lightly steamed thin green beans) gluten free crisps or gluten free crackers or toast.

AVOCADO AND CANELLINI/WHITE KIDNEY BEAN DIP WITH PINE NUTS

Yet another variation on the hummus theme but with a greater emphasis on the avocado.

INGREDIENTS
SERVES 4

2 ripe avocados

2 level tbsp canned cannellini beans

½ – 1 ½ small hot red chillies, deseeded and chopped very small

sea salt

juice 1 lemon (optional)

2 tbsp pine nuts

METHOD

In a liquidiser or food processor whizz the avocados with the beans until smooth.

Add salt and the chopped chilli, gradually whizzing briefly between each addition and tasting all the time, until you reach the degree of spiciness that you want.

Add the lemon juice if you are using it and whizz briefly.

When you are happy with the flavour, add the pine nuts and whizz again so that the pine nuts get broken up but not puréed.

Serve with crudités or gluten-free breadsticks or crackers.

AJWAR

Ajwar is a Yugoslavian pâté made with the red peppers so beloved in south eastern Europe. Purists will skin the peppers by submerging them in hot oil till they blister, and look askance at the addition of aubergine, let alone brown bread. However, skinning the peppers is a slow and fiddly business which I feel is scarcely justified by the marginal improvement in the flavour, and the pâté is so rich in its native form that a little dilution does not go amiss. It is delicious served either with fresh gluten-free brown bread or toast, or as a dip with crudités.

INGREDIENTS
SERVES 4

4 thickish slices of aubergine/eggplant

approx. 2 tbsp olive oil

2 large red bell peppers, deseeded and roughly chopped

2 large cloves garlic

2 thick slices gluten-free brown bread

sea salt and freshly ground black pepper

METHOD

Fry the aubergine slices in the oil until they are just brown on each side.

Put all the ingredients – fried aubergine, peppers, garlic, and bread – in a food processor and purée them.

The pâté should not be totally smooth when puréed; rather it should have the texture of a country terrine.

Season lightly with sea salt and freshly ground black pepper and leave for a couple of hours for the flavours to mature.

Adjust the seasoning again to taste before serving with fresh gluten-free brown bread or toast, or as a dip with crudités.

AUBERGINE/EGGPLANT AND NUT BUTTER PÂTÉ

Aubergine/eggplant pâtés on their own can be very sloppy — and nut and seed butters tend to be very solid — so combining them seems the ideal answer. I use an almond and cashew nut butter, but you could use peanut, sesame, pumpkin, or any other nut butter that you fancy.

INGREDIENTS
SERVES 4 - 6

1 large aubergine/eggplant

½ head (approx. 6 cloves) of fresh garlic

3 tbsp of nut or seed butter of your choice

sea salt and freshly ground black pepper

METHOD

Wipe the aubergine/eggplant and cut into large chunks.

Peel the garlic cloves and halve.

Put both into a steamer and steam for 10 minutes or until the aubergine/eggplant is quite soft.

Transfer to a food processor and add the nut or seed butter.

Purée thoroughly, adding extra nut or seed butter if the pâté is too sloppy.

Season to taste and serve with crudités or gluten-free bread or crackers.

PASTA AND PIZZA

Free-from fusilli with chard and leeks

Anna's chickpea or buckwheat pasta with garlic and chilli

Asparagus rice-noodle stir fry

Mac 'n' cheese

Fresh cherry tomato sauce

Katherine's kale and cashew nut pesto

Creamy leak sauce for corn-based pasta

Rice and seed 'pizza' base

Pizza toppings:

Red pepper and caper

Salsa and tofu

Mushroom and artichoke heart

Gluten-free pasta based on everything from seaweed to chickpeas is now so good and so varied that those on gluten-free diets are positively spoiled for choice.

However, depending on their base, the textures and flavours can be very different, so you need to match your pasta and sauce with care. A delicate sauce such as the creamy leek one would work really well with a corn, rice, or corn and rice-based pasta whereas a more vigorous chickpea and buckwheat-based pasta would do far better with a more pungent sauce such as garlic and chilli.

FREE-FROM FUSILLI WITH CHARD AND LEEKS

A very simple but delicious pasta dish. Ideally use a corn, or corn and rice-based pasta as you do not want the flavour of the pasta to overwhelm the leeks.

Traditionally this dish would be sprinkled with Parmesan before serving and you can certainly sprinkle it with a grated vegan cheese, although I don't really think it needs it.

INGREDIENTS
SERVES 4

6 tbsp olive oil

3 medium to large, leeks, trimmed and finely sliced

250g/10 oz fresh, young chard

300ml/10fl oz/1 ¼ cups gluten and wheat free vegetable stock

300g/12 oz gluten/wheat free fusilli – corn or corn and rice based

sea salt and freshly ground black pepper

finely grated, strong flavoured vegan cheese (optional)

METHOD

Heat 4 tablespoons of the oil in a large flat pan and add the leeks. Stir around and sweat very gently, without burning, for 15–20 minutes or until they are quite soft.

Meanwhile, wash the chard and remove the stalks. Chop the stalks roughly then chop the leaves quite roughly but keep them separate from the stalks

Add the chard stalks to the leek and cook for another 3–4 minutes, then add the leaves and continue to cook gently for a further 7–8 minutes or until the leaves are cooked. Season to taste.

Meanwhile season 1 litre/2 pints/4 ¼ cups of water generously with salt and bring it to the boil. Add the pasta and cook according to the instructions on the pack (depending on which gluten-free pasta you use cooking times will differ quite dramatically).

Drain un-thoroughly (there should still be some water clinging to the pasta) and mix it thoroughly into the chard and leek. Lightly mix in the remaining 2 tbsp of olive oil.

Serve at once with and plenty of freshly ground black pepper and grated vegan cheese if you want to use it.

ANNA'S CHICKPEA OR BUCKWHEAT PASTA WITH GARLIC AND CHILLI

A lovely simple recipe from the *'Simply Italian, Simply Gluten Free'* book I published with Anna Del Conte last year. As Anna says, it is a robust, piquant sauce, ideal for robust pasta like buckwheat or chickpea. You need to adjust the amount of chilli to your taste.

INGREDIENTS
SERVES 4

400g/14 oz chickpea or buckwheat fusilli or penne

7 tbsp olive oil

4 large garlic cloves, finely chopped

1–2 fresh chillies, cores and seeds removed, flesh chopped finely

2 sprigs fresh rosemary, leaves finely chopped

2 tsp lemon juice

METHOD

Cook the pasta in plenty of well salted, boiling water according to the instructions on the pack.

While the pasta is cooking, heat the olive oil in large frying pan. When hot throw in the chopped garlic, chilli and rosemary and fry, stirring constantly for one 1 minute and pressing the ingredients to release the juices.

Drain the pasta and turn it immediately into the frying pan. Now stir it over and over so that all the pasta pieces get thoroughly dressed.

Sprinkle with lemon juice, stir again and serve at once, straight from the pan.

ASPARAGUS AND RICE-NOODLE STIR FRY

A tasty stir fry given lots of texture by the addition of the crunchy peas to the softened vegetables and the super soft rice noodles. Make sure you use a good quality miso as it will add lots of flavour to the dish.

INGREDIENTS
SERVES 4

12 stalks of asparagus cut into 2cm/1 inch, pieces

250ml/9fl oz/1 cup gluten-free miso

2 tbsp coconut or stir fry oil

50g/2 oz knob of peeled fresh ginger, chopped small

4 large cloves garlic, peeled and sliced

1–2 hot small green chillies (depending on how hot you want your stir fry) deseeded and chopped small

1 medium red bell pepper,

deseeded and sliced finely

300g/12 oz rice noodles

2 handfuls of mangetouts or sugar snap peas, trimmed and halved or cut in thirds

salt

3 tbsp sweet rice wine

2–3 tbsp wheat-free tamari

juice 3–4 limes

6 spring onions/scallions, sliced lengthways and cut into 3 or 4 pieces

METHOD

Steam the asparagus over boiling water for 3–5 minutes only. You want them to remain crunchy but to take the chewiness out of them.

Make up 250ml/9fl oz/1 cup of gluten-free miso.

Heat the oil in a wok and gently cook the ginger, garlic, and chilli along with the pepper slices for 5 minutes or until they are all starting to soften.

Meanwhile, break the rice noodles into roughly 8 cm/3-inch lengths, and add them to a large pan of fast boiling water. Stir well to prevent them clumping and then boil briskly for 4–5 minutes until they are no longer chewy but are not mushy. Drain.

Add the mange tout/sugar snaps and the noodles to the vegetables in the wok.

Add salt, rice wine and tamari to taste, mix well and cook for a further minute

Add the asparagus, mix gently so as not to break the asparagus, cook for another minute then season with the lime juice to taste.

Serve at once, sprinkled with the chopped spring onions/scallions.

MAC 'N' CHEESE

Mac 'n' cheese is definitely a challenge for the vegan cook. The original is so heavily dependent on dairy products (butter, milk, and cheese) that replicating them successfully can be difficult. This is especially relevant as far as the cheese goes as, good though many vegan cheeses now are, none of them really have that flavour edge that you get from a mature hard dairy cheese. In this recipe I have replaced that kick with a good helping of mustard, both French and English.

INGREDIENTS
SERVES 6

300g /12 oz gluten free macaroni of your choice

600ml/1 ¼ pint/2 ½ cups soya, oat, nut, or coconut milk – whichever you can tolerate and prefer. The milk you use will very slightly change the flavour of the dish but not dramatically.

300g/12 oz block of strong 'cheddar style' vegan cheese (Don't buy ready grated as it has often been coated to stop it sticking.)

50g/2 oz vegan/milk free spread or coconut oil

25g/1 oz gluten-free plain flour mix

2 heaped tsp gluten-free English mustard powder

5 tbsp gluten-free wholegrain French mustard

sea salt and freshly ground black pepper

50g/2 oz gluten-free breadcrumbs or crushed plain gluten-free crisps

METHOD
Heat the oven to 180°C/350°F/Gas Mark 4.

Cook the macaroni in plenty of fast boiling well salted water for a couple of minutes less than it says on the pack. (Cooking times will differ depending on the base of the pasta.) You want it to be almost cooked by not quite so that it finishes cooking in the oven.

Heat the milk to just below boiling.

Grate the cheese.

Melt the spread or coconut oil in, preferably, a non-stick pan. Gradually add the flour with the English mustard powder and stir well till you get a smooth paste.

Slowly add the milk, stirring all the time, and cook gently until the sauce thickens.

Add the French mustard and 250g/10 oz of the cheese. Stir well and cook gently for 3–4 minutes until the cheese has melted into the sauce.

Season to taste.

Check the consistency of the sauce — it should just coat the back of a spoon so if too thick add a little more milk. You don't want it to be too thick as it will thicken up in the oven.

Stir in the macaroni and made sure it is all well coated, then turn into an oven proof dish.

Mix the breadcrumbs or crisps with the remaining cheese and spread over the top of the dish.

Bake uncovered for 35-40 minutes or until it is bubbling and lightly tanned on top.

Serve at once with a large green salad.

FRESH CHERRY TOMATO SAUCE

A simple, fresh tomato sauce to be used with pasta or gnocchi.

INGREDIENTS
SERVES 6

4 tbsp olive oil

2 small onions, peeled and finely chopped

1 large head fennel, chopped small

4 heaped tsp dried oregano

1 kg 200g/2lb 10 oz fresh cherry tomatoes, quartered

1 ½ glasses dry white wine

sea salt and freshly ground black pepper

finely grated hard vegan cheese (optional)

METHOD

Heat the oil in heavy saucepan and gently fry the onions, fennel, and oregano for 10 minutes or until well softened.

Add the tomatoes and wine, bring to the boil, cover, and reduce the heat to a simmer.

Simmer for 25–30 minutes or until the tomatoes are totally broken down and the fennel quite soft.

If you like your sauce 'bitty', just season to taste and serve immediately with the gnocchi or pasta of your choice.

If you prefer your sauce smoother, purée in a food processor, and then season to taste.

Reheat and serve with pasta or gnocchi. Sprinkle with vegan cheese if you are using it..

KATHERINE'S KALE AND CASHEW NUT PESTO

Kale takes on a brilliant green colour when cooked. The cashew nuts add a little creaminess to balance the peppery kale. Delicious with pasta or to add to sandwiches or salads.

INGREDIENTS
approx. 200g/8 oz bag of kale

1 clove garlic

6 tbsp olive oil

juice ½ lemon

2 handfuls cashew nuts

salt and pepper

METHOD

Wash the kale and remove any large stalks — these will not blend and will make the pesto hairy!

Either steam the kale or boil in salted water for a few minutes.

Drain and place in a food processor.

Place all the other ingredients in and blend until smooth.

Season with salt and pepper to taste.

Add more oil if you want a softer consistency.

Stir it through any gluten free pasta.

CREAMY LEEK SAUCE FOR CORN-BASED PASTA

You need to be patient with this sauce to ensure that the leeks are literally cooked to a mush — but a very delicious mush! I do not think that it needs either salt or cheese — just lots of freshly ground black pepper — but taste and decide for yourself.

INGREDIENTS
SERVES 4

4 large leeks – approx. 600g/1½ lbs when trimmed of their coarse green leaves

2 level tsp fennel seeds

6 tbsp olive oil

400ml/14fl oz/1 2/3 cups gluten-free vegetable stock

200ml/7fl oz/generous ¾ cup dry white wine

4 tbsp plain coconut or soy yogurt

sea salt and freshly ground black pepper

300g/12 oz gluten-free corn or corn and rice-based spaghetti

vegan hard cheese (optional)

METHOD

Trim the leeks of their coarse green leaves and outer layers and slice very thinly. If necessary, wash under running water and dry with kitchen towel/paper.

Lightly crush the fennel seeds with the end of a rolling pin or in a pestle and mortar. Heat the oil in a heavy pan and add the fennel seeds and leeks and sauté gently for 10-15 minutes or until they are really soft.

Add the stock and wine, bring to the boil then turn down the heat, cover, and simmer very gently for 40-50 minutes or until they have all but turned into mush. Stir in the yogurt and season with salt, if needed.

Meanwhile, cook the spaghetti in plenty of well salted, boiling water according to the directions on the pack. Drain, retaining a small amount of the cooking water. Use this to thin the sauce slightly.

Pile the pasta into four large bowls and spoon the sauce over each. Grind over lots of black pepper and sprinkle with cheese if you are using it.

RICE AND SEED 'PIZZA' BASE

This is not a real pizza base, but it works well as an alternative for traditional pizza and for any pizza style toppings. If you like it quite soft you can use it immediately. Alternatively, you can dry it out in the oven before adding the topping.

INGREDIENTS
MAKES A 25CM/10 INCH 'PIZZA'

100g/4 oz sushi or sticky rice

500ml/18fl oz/2 cups gluten-free miso or gluten-free vegetable stock

1 level tbsp hulled sesame or hulled hemp seeds

1 level tbsp chia seeds

METHOD

Heat the oven to 170°C/325°F/Gas Mark 3.

Rinse the rice in cold water and then soak it in the miso or stock for 30 minutes.

Add the seeds, bring to the boil, in a non-stick saucepan if possible, cover and simmer for 15 minutes. The rice should be very soft.

Turn off the heat and leave covered for 10 minutes.

Cover a baking tray with oiled foil.

Then spread the rice mixture over it with a palette knife or spatula as evenly as you can and bake for 30 minutes to dry out slightly.

PIZZA TOPPINGS

A selection of toppings that you could use with the rice base above or with a standard gluten free pizza base.

RED PEPPER AND CAPER

INGREDIENTS
ENOUGH FOR A 25CM/10-INCH 'PIZZA'

2 tbsp olive oil

2 small or 1 large leek, finely sliced

2 red Romana peppers/sweet pointed, deseeded and finely sliced

2–4 red chillies, depending on how hot you want your pizza, deseeded, and very finely chopped

10–15 plum tomatoes

100g/4 oz vegan hard cheese, grated

6–8 tsp capers in either brine or olive oil

freshly ground black pepper

METHOD

Heat the oven to 190°C/375°F/Gas Mark 5.

Heat the oil in a wide pan and gently fry the leeks, peppers, and chillies for 4–5 minutes until they are just starting to soften. Make sure they do not burn.

Slice the tomatoes and spread the slices over the 'pizza' base and cover them with the vegan cheese.

Spread the pepper mixture over the top and sprinkle over the capers

Bake for 15 minutes, grind over lots of black pepper and serve at once.

SALSA AND TOFU

INGREDIENTS
ENOUGH FOR A 25CM/10-INCH 'PIZZA'

1 level tbsp coconut or olive oil

1 medium onion, peeled and sliced thinly

2 large cloves garlic, peeled and thinly sliced

100g/4 oz oyster (or other) mushrooms, chopped roughly

1 x 250g/9 oz jar of your favourite salsa — check ingredients

4 large handfuls of baby spinach, washed and well dried

100g/4 oz plain tofu crumbled into smallish pieces

50g/2 oz cashew nuts, fresh or roasted

METHOD

Heat the oven to 190°C/375°F/Gas Mark 5.

Heat the oil in a wide pan, add the onion and garlic and cook gently for 8–10 minutes or until they are starting to soften.

Add the mushrooms and continue to cook for a further few minutes.

Spread the salsa thickly over the pizza base then spread the spinach leaves over the salsa.

Spread the tofu over the spinach then cover it with the onion and mushroom mixture.

Sprinkle over the cashew nuts.

Cook for 15 minutes and serve at once.

MUSHROOM AND ARTICHOKE HEART

The lemon juice is not essential - just adds a little bite!

INGREDIENTS
ENOUGH FOR A 25CM/10-INCH 'PIZZA'

2 tbsp olive oil

150g/6 oz chestnut or button mushrooms, wiped and sliced

6-8 tinned artichoke hearts, drained and quartered

juice 1 small lemon (optional)

sea salt and freshly ground black pepper

METHOD

Heat the oil in a heavy, deep pan and briskly fry the mushrooms for 3–5 minutes or until the juices run.

Spoon them over the pizza base.

Arrange the artichoke heart quarters over the top, squeeze over the lemon juice if you are using it and season generously with sea salt and freshly ground black pepper.

Bake for 15 minutes in a hot oven and serve at once.

VEGETABLE DISHES

||||||||||||||||||||||||||||||||

Cauliflower, tofu, garlic, and coriander stir fry

Stir fried broccoli with tofu and cashews

Celeriac mash with cavolo nero, garlic
and smoked tofu

Roasted red onion and beetroot/beet with
sweet potato and ginger

Cavolo nero with beetroot/beet leaves/greens

Katherine's roast carrot Moroccan stew

Layered vegetables with pecans

Anna's cavolo nero and sautéed potatoes with
chilli and garlic

Okra with onions

Carrot and leek tart with ginger

Parsnips with caramelised onion

Sweet potato chips/fries

I love vegetables and am happy to eat almost any combination of them, steamed, stir fried, sautéed, for almost every meal. My principle is to buy anything that looks nice in the market or the greengrocers and stick it in the fridge and then, when I want a meal, to choose whatever combination appeals at the moment, cook them adding back pepper, seeds, nuts, herbs, chilli flakes as the mood moves me. Or indeed, sometimes, I just chop them and eat them raw.

Usually, I cook them on the hob because it is quicker, but if you are using the oven anyhow, then popping them in the oven is great.

The recipes below have formalised a few of these combinations but, as with making soup, I really encourage you to experiment. Some combinations will work better than others but you will rarely have a failure.

The one golden rule is to undercook rather than over cook. You can always put them back for a bit longer but once they are overcooked, all is lost. To minimise the chance of overcooking, I steam vegetables rather than boiling them; a steamer is much more forgiving.

CAULIFLOWER, TOFU, GARLIC AND CORIANDER STIR FRY

A very tasty combination and delightfully quick to throw together!

INGREDIENTS
SERVES 4

2 tbsp coconut oil

2 small hot red chillies, deseeded and chopped finely

Approx. 50g/2 oz trimmed fresh ginger, sliced into thin matchsticks

4 large cloves garlic, peeled and sliced thinly

2 small or 1 large red Romano pepper, deseeded and sliced thinly

400g/1 lb fresh cauliflower florets, cut into small bite size pieces

200g/8 oz fresh firm tofu cut into fat matchsticks

400g/1 lb beansprouts

100g/4 oz peppered cashew nuts

4 tbsp gluten-free soy sauce

2 tbsp mirin

2 large handfuls fresh coriander, roughly chopped

METHOD

Heat the oil in a wok or a wide frying pan and add the chillies, ginger, garlic, and Romano peppers.

Fry fairly gently for 10 minutes, making sure that nothing burns.

Add the cauliflower florets and the tofu, mix well, cover the pan, and continue to cook for 5 minutes to just soften the cauliflower.

Remove the lid and add the beansprouts and cashews, with the soy sauce and mirin.

Mix well and continue to cook for a further three minutes.

Serve at once liberally sprinkled with the chopped coriander.

STIR FRIED BROCCOLI WITH TOFU AND CASHEWS

This is one of Katherine's tastier recipes. If you think of it in time, leave the tofu to marinate for a few hours before you actually make the dish. Depending on hunger levels you can serve it on its own or with boiled rice or gluten-free noodles.

INGREDIENTS
SERVES 4

4 tsp sesame oil

4 tbsp wheat free tamari

approx. 25g/1 oz of finely grated fresh ginger

600g/1lb 5 oz block of firm plain tofu, cubed

700g/1lb 8 oz tender stem broccoli/ broccolini

1 large onion

2 small, red chillies, deseeded and finely chopped

300g/12 oz shiitake mushrooms

4 tbsp oil

150g/6 oz salted cashew nuts to serve

METHOD

Mix the sesame oil, tamari, and grated ginger together.

Gently stir in the tofu and leave to marinate while you prepare the other ingredients.

Bring a large saucepan of salted water to the boil.

Cut the broccoli lengthwise into separate stems and cook for 3 minutes. Drain and set aside.

Cut the onion in half and then slice, not too thinly.

Finely chop the chilli and roughly chop the mushrooms.

Heat the oil in a wok and gently stir fry the tofu, including marinade, along with the mushrooms, chilli, and onion.

After a few minutes, add the broccoli/broccolini to warm through.

Top with the cashew nuts and serve alone or with rice or noodles.

CELERIAC MASH WITH CAVOLO NERO, GARLIC AND SMOKED TOFU

A nice warming combination. If possible, make the cavolo nero mixture at least a few hours before you want to eat it to leave it time to rest and for the flavours to amalgamate and mature.

INGREDIENTS
SERVES 4

100g/4 oz cavolo nero or other dark coloured kale, thick stems trimmed off. Weight should be after the stems have been trimmed.

3 tbsp coconut oil or 3 tbsp olive oil

3–4 large cloves garlic, peeled and very thinly sliced

200g/8 oz smoked tofu — be sure that it is gluten free

1 x 400g/14 oz can tomatoes

180ml/6fl oz/ 3/4 cup red wine

sea salt and freshly ground black pepper

1 large celeriac root — approx. 1 kg/2 lbs when trimmed

3–4 tbsp soya or coconut yogurt

METHOD

Trim and wash the cavolo nero or kale and steam it for 8–10 minutes. It should be almost, but not quite, cooked.

Heat the oil in a wide pan and gently fry the sliced garlic. It should start to soften but not change colour. Add the steamed cavolo nero, stir well and cook for a couple of minutes.

Cut the tofu into 2 cm/1-inch cubes and add to the cavolo nero along with the canned tomatoes and the wine.

Season fairly generously, bring to the boil cover and simmer very gently for 15 minutes then adjust the seasoning to taste. Leave to rest for a few hours or even overnight.

Cut the celeriac into approximately 2 cm/1-inch cubes, and steam for 15–20 minutes or until they are soft. Purée in a liquidiser or food processor, adding the yogurt until you get a soft but not sloppy consistency. Season to taste with salt and pepper.

To serve, reheat the cavolo nero mixture and check seasoning. Pile the celeriac purée in the middle of a warmed serving dish then spoon cavolo nero mixture on top. Serve at once.

ROASTED RED ONION AND BEETROOT/ BEET, SWEET POTATO AND GINGER

An amazingly coloured dish of roast vegetables – so easy – and so delicious!

I am afraid that I am a bit of a ginger freak, so it does manage to creep into a lot of my recipes. It is delicious in these roast vegetables, but they are also delicious coated with herby, rather than gingery olive oil.

INGREDIENTS
SERVES 4

4 medium red onions, peeled but left whole

4 medium raw beetroot/beets with their leaves and stems, if possible – scrubbed and halved

2–4 sweet potatoes, depending on size, peeled, and halved or quartered

1 sizeable knob of fresh ginger, its size depends on how keen you are on ginger – peeled (optional)

or 2 heaped tsp dried Herbes de Provence or mixed herbs

approx. 6 tbsp olive oil

sea salt and freshly ground black pepper

100g/4 oz of trimmed curly kale or mature spinach leaves, chopped, or 70g/3 oz finely sliced Savoy cabbage if you cannot get the beetroot/beets with their leaves and stalks

METHOD

Heat the oven to 180°C/350°F/Gas mark 4.

Scatter the onions, beetroot/beets, and sweet potato around a baking dish.

If you have the beetroot/beet stalks, chop them into 5cm/2-inch pieces reserving the leaves, and scatter over the vegetables.

Grate the ginger, or stir the herbs, into the olive oil and mix well, then use to coat the vegetables allowing any extra to run into the bottom of the dish

Cover the vegetables lightly with foil and bake for approximately 45 minutes or until they are nearly soft. Turn the vegetables every 15 minutes to ensure that they are well coated in the gingery or herby oil.

Remove the foil, turn the vegetables one more time and spread the chopped beetroot/beet leaves, kale, spinach, or cabbage over them. Lay the foil lightly over the top and return to the oven for a final 15 minutes before serving.

CAVOLO NERO WITH BEETROOT/ BEET LEAVES/GREENS

Very dark cabbages can be slightly bitter but adding apple just takes off that bitter edge. If you cannot get cavolo nero, you could just use curly kale.

INGREDIENTS
SERVES 4

2 tbsp olive oil

1 large onion, peeled and sliced

1 large cooking apple, Bramley if possible, wiped and chopped small, with its skin on

sea salt

300g/12 oz cavolo nero

150g/6 oz curly kale

150g/6 oz beetroot/beet leaves/greens with stalks, if you can find them — if not, 300g/12 oz assorted kales

2–3 tbsp water

freshly ground black pepper

METHOD

Heat the oil in a deep pan and add the onion and apple with a pinch of salt to help prevent it burning.

Fry gently for 5–8 minutes or until the onion is quite soft — but watch it carefully as it will burn very easily.

Wash all the greens and remove any coarse stalks. Shake dry, leaving a fair amount of water on the leaves, then chop roughly.

Add to the onion mix, cover, and cook gently for 5–10 minutes or until the greens are cooked but retain a little crunch. If they appear to be drying up, add a little water – the mixture should be moist without being wet.

Season to taste before serving.

KATHERINE'S ROAST CARROT MOROCCAN STEW

A lovely golden, warming, spicy stew — both in looks and in flavour. It was one of Katherine's favourite family meals. You can serve it with rice, crusty gluten free bread or green vegetables.

INGREDIENTS
SERVES 4

3 large or 4 smaller carrots

2 tbsp olive oil

1 medium onion, chopped

1 large clove of garlic, crushed

1 level tsp ground cumin

1 level tsp ground ginger

½ level tsp ground turmeric

½ level tsp cinnamon

1 level tsp paprika

400g/14 oz can chopped tomatoes

400g/14 oz can chickpeas, drained and rinsed

1–2 tsp honey

sea salt and freshly ground black pepper

300g or 4 large handfuls of spinach

optional: coconut or soya yogurt to serve

METHOD

Preheat the oven to 180°C/350°F/Gas mark 4.

Scrub the carrots and chop them into 1 cm/½-inch slices. If the carrots are very large, cut the slices in half, place them in a baking tray and coat in 1 tablespoon of olive oil.

Cook for about 30 minutes until lightly browned and soft enough to prod a fork through.

Meanwhile, heat the other tablespoon of oil in a large saucepan.

Add the onion and cook gently for a few minutes until softened then add the garlic, cumin, ginger, turmeric, cinnamon and paprika. Cook for 2 minutes, stirring constantly.

Next add the tomatoes. Fill the can ¾ full of water and pour in. Cook for about 15 minutes, stirring occasionally.

Stir in the chickpeas and honey (start with 1 teaspoon and add to taste) Season to taste with salt and pepper.

Pile the spinach on top and put a lid on the saucepan and cook for a few minutes until the spinach has wilted. Stir the spinach through and add the roasted carrots.

Serve with rice and a dollop of yogurt on top.

LAYERED VEGETABLES WITH PECANS

Delicious and filling. The ideal November dish.

INGREDIENTS
SERVES 4

500g/1 lb peeled celeriac

2–3 sharp eating apples, depending on size, cored but not peeled

6 tbsp olive oil

2 level tsp fennel seeds

1 medium onion, peeled and sliced

200g/8 oz Savoy or other curly green cabbage

150g/6 oz chestnut mushrooms, wiped and sliced

100g/4 oz pecan nuts or if you cannot eat pecan nuts, pumpkin seeds

50g/2 oz hazelnuts, ground small in a food processor, or, if you cannot eat hazelnuts, sesame, or poppy seeds

sea salt and freshly ground black pepper

METHOD
Grate the celeriac and the apples coarsely. Heat 2 tablespoons of the oil in a heavy pan and add the celeriac, apple, and fennel seeds.

Stir well and fry for a few minutes then cover and sweat for 25–30 minutes or until the celeriac is quite soft. Season to taste.

Peel and slice the onions thickly.

Heat 2 tablespoons of oil in a separate pan, add the onions and fry gently until they are nearly transparent

Meanwhile, wash and slice the cabbage thinly. Add to the onion, stir well, cover the pan, and cook gently for 15 minutes or until the cabbage is nearly cooked.

Season to taste.

Heat the rest of the oil in a third pan and cook the mushrooms briskly for several minutes then add the pecan nuts, or pumpkin seeds. Continue to cook until the juices run from the mushrooms.

Spoon just over half the celeriac mixture into the bottom of a large ovenproof dish and flatten out.

Cover with the cabbage and onion mixture, then the mushroom and pecans.

Spread the remains of the celeriac over the top and sprinkle with the hazelnuts, or sesame seeds.

Reheat, if necessary, in the oven or toast lightly under a grill/broiler to roast the topping lightly.

Serve at once with a green vegetable or salad.

ANNA'S CAVOLO NERO AND SAUTÉED POTATOES WITH CHILLI AND GARLIC

Another of Anna's wonderfully simple but totally delicious dishes from our '*Simply Italian, Simply Gluten*' free book. Anna says the potatoes lend substance to the cavolo nero and the cavolo nero lends its peculiar bitter cabbagey flavour to the potatoes — a perfect combination.

If you cannot find cavolo nero use any dark kale.

INGREDIENTS
SERVES 4

4 large waxy potatoes, approx. 700g/1lb 8 oz

10 cavolo nero leaves

1 tbsp olive oil

2 garlic cloves

2 pinches chilli flakes

sea salt

METHOD

Scrub the potatoes and put them, still in their skins, in a saucepan. Cover with cold water, add 1 tablespoon of sea salt and cook at a lively simmer until just tender when tested with the point of a small knife.

Lift them out of the water with a slotted spoon (reserve the water) and place in a colander until cool enough to peel. Then peel and cut into large bite sized chunks.

Remove the tough stalks from the cavolo nero, wash the leaves and cut into strips.

Bring the potato water back to the boil and add the cavolo nero. Boil until tender — it will take 10–15 minutes. Drain well

While the cavolo nero is cooking, heat the oil in a large frying pan and add the garlic and chilli flakes. Sauté until just golden and add to the potatoes.

Mix well for a minute or two then add the cavolo nero and continue cooking for 5 minutes, turning all the time.

Taste and add sea salt if necessary, before serving.

OKRA WITH ONIONS

The complaint usually levelled at okra is that it is too slimy but, cooked this way, it never gets a chance to get slimy — and is delicious.

INGREDIENTS
SERVES 4

4 tbsp olive oil

2 heaped tsp cumin powder

2 large onions, peeled and chopped roughly

4–6 cloves garlic, depending on size, peeled, and finely sliced

250g/10 oz okra, topped and tailed

METHOD

Heat the oil in a heavy, wide pan with the cumin.

Add the onion and garlic and fry very gently for 15–20 minutes or until the onion is quite cooked.

Slice the okra lengthways into four or six matchsticks, depending on size

Add to the onion, increase the heat slightly and cook very briefly — no more than a minute maximum

Turn into a dish and serve at once.

CARROT AND LEEK TART WITH GINGER

Carrot and ginger soup is a classic — but how about carrot and ginger tart?

INGREDIENTS
SERVES 4

3 tbsp olive oil

300g/12 oz carrots, scrubbed and sliced in thin rounds

3 medium leeks, trimmed and finely sliced

40–50g/1 ½–2 oz ginger root, trimmed and cut into thin matchsticks

150g/6 oz gram/chickpea flour, sieved

100g/4 oz rice flour

1 level tsp xanthan gum

125g/5 oz dairy-free spread

80–100ml chilled water

150g/6 oz fresh spinach leaves

sea salt and freshly ground black pepper

juice 1 lemon

METHOD

Heat the oven to 180°C/350°F/Gas mark 4.

Heat the oil in a wide pan and add the carrots, leeks, and ginger root. Sweat very gently with the lid on for 30–40 minutes.

Meanwhile, make the pastry by whizzing the flour and the xanthan gum in a food processor with the dairy-free spread until it is the texture of breadcrumbs.

Tip out of the processor into a bowl and add the water, pulling the flour into the centre and quickly kneading into ball — do not over work.

On a floured board, roll out the pastry and line a 20cm/8-inch flan case. Line with foil and weigh the foil down with beans or rice.

Bake for 25 minutes. Remove the foil and beans and cook for a further ten minutes to crisp up the bottom of the pastry case.

Add the spinach leaves to the carrot mix, allow them to wilt then mix them in.

Season with salt, pepper and lemon juice then spoon into the flan case.

Serve warm or at room temperature.

PARSNIP WITH CARAMELISED ONION

If you like onions at all, this is a totally delicious dish, but you must be patient. The secret is to cook the onions very slowly so that they become soft, golden, and caramelised. As they do so their sweetness comes out which combines naturally with the sweetness of the parsnips. I love this but if you think it might be a little cloying you can add a kick with a little chilli.

Because the onions are quite rich, I think the flan is best served with a plain steamed green vegetable (chard, spinach, cabbage, or Brussels sprouts) or a salad.

INGREDIENTS
SERVES 4

8 tbsp olive oil

6 large (and I mean large!) onions, peeled and thinly sliced

3 small hot chillies (optional), deseeded and finely chopped

3–4 large parsnips, peeled or scrubbed and sliced thinly

75g/3 oz pine nuts

sea salt and freshly ground black pepper

METHOD

Heat the olive oil gently in a large sauté pan and add the finely sliced onions and stir well around.

If you are using them, add the chillies.

Sauté very gently over a low heat for 30–45 minutes, stirring regularly to stop the onions catching. You want them to cook very slowly and gently and to gradually turn golden and caramelise.

While the onions are cooking, steam the sliced parsnips until really soft. They should take 8–10 minutes but it will depend on the thickness of the slices.

Dry fry the pine nuts until they are golden being careful that they do not burn.

When the vegetables are cooked, spread the parsnips out in the bottom of a warmed serving dish and season fairly generously with sea salt and freshly ground black pepper.

Spoon the caramelised onions over the top and spread out evenly and top with the toasted pine nuts. Serve at once with a green vegetable or salad.

SWEET POTATO CHIPS/FRIES

So simple to make – and so tasty....

INGREDIENTS

1 medium size sweet potato per person

1 – 2 tbsp cornflour/corn starch or gluten-free flour

olive oil

sea salt and freshly ground black pepper

paprika, cumin or rosemary – optional

METHOD

Preheat the oven to 220°C/450°F/Gas Mark 6.

Peel the sweet potatoes then slice lengthways — around 1 cm/½ inch thick.

Slice the disks into chips/fries as thin or thick as you like.

Try to keep the chip/fry size as even as you can so they cook at a similar rate.

Place the potatoes in a bowl and coat in the flour.

Drizzle over some olive oil and coat evenly.

Add the salt and pepper, paprika, cumin or rosemary, and any other seasoning of your choice.

Mix thoroughly and spread out on a baking tray.

Cook for 10–20 minutes (depending on chip/fry size) until browned and then carefully turn them over. Keep watching them as you don't want them to burn.

Cook for another 10–20 minutes until nicely brown.

Serve immediately.

PULSE BASED DISHES

Braised chicory with lentils, butter beans and red peppers

Lentil, bean, and sausage pot

Katherine's cabbage with chickpeas and tahini dressing

Swede/rutabaga and chickpea mush

Flageolet, fennel, and chard pot meal with green peppercorns

Puy lentils with okra and coriander/cilantro

Mushroom and tender stem broccoli with Puy lentils

While vegetables on their own are delicious and offer a wealth of options, combining them with pulses adds not only another whole layer of exciting possibilities, but a lot more in terms of cost-effective bulk — extremely useful if you are in the business of filling hollow legs.

Pulses are the dried seeds of legumes including beans, peas, chickpeas, vetches, and lentils and while some can just be cooked within the dish (lentils, for example), most need pre-soaking and pre-cooking — a step that you can avoid by using canned pulses which have already been cooked.

Canned pulses are hugely convenient and work well in dishes in which there are lots of other ingredients. However, when they are the primary ingredients, or when you have the time, the taste is deeper and the texture more interesting if you soak and cook the beans yourself. This requires no expertise beyond thinking ahead far enough to soak them overnight and leave 2-3 hours for boiling them. However, knowing that few people will have time for that, in most of the recipes below I have use canned pulses.

BRAISED CHICORY WITH LENTILS, BUTTER BEANS AND RED PEPPERS

A rather unusual but tasty combination. Blanching the chicory briefly in acidulated water — water with lemon juice added — just takes off the slightly bitter edge that some people find unpleasant.

INGREDIENTS
SERVES 4

1 heaped tbsp coconut oil or 2 tbsp olive oil

1 large or 2 medium onions, finely chopped

1 large stick celery, finely chopped

2 Romano red peppers, cut into long, thin matchsticks

several sprigs of fresh thyme or 2 tsp of dried

100g/4 oz red lentils

500ml/generous 18fl oz/2 cups gluten and wheat free vegetable stock

1 x 400g/14 oz can butter beans, drained

1 small head choi sum or other small Chinese green leaf, or a handful of chard or spinach, chopped roughly

4 heads chicory/endive

½ lemon

sea salt and freshly ground black pepper

a large handful of parsley, flat-leaf, if possible

METHOD

Heat the oil in a deep, wide pan and add the onion, celery, peppers, and the thyme. Fry gently for 15 minutes or until all are well softened.

Add the red lentils and the stock. Bring to the boil, cover, and simmer for 10 minutes, then uncover and continue to cook for a further 5 minutes or until the lentils are totally 'mushed' into the stock to form a thick sauce.

Add the butter beans and the choi sum, chard or spinach and stir gently keeping the heat low — just enough to heat through the beans and wilt the greens.

Meanwhile bring a pan of water just big enough to hold the chicory/endive to the boil.

Trim any outside leaves off the chicory/endive and halve them lengthways. Squeeze a little lemon juice into the water and then drop in the chicory heads. Leave for no more than a minute and remove with a slotted spoon.

Add the chicory/endive to the pot and stir gently to incorporate it without breaking the heads up too much. Season to taste.

Just before serving add lots of roughly chopped parsley.

Serve with a green salad.

LENTIL, BEAN AND SAUSAGE POT

A warming and filling classic bean pot for a winter evening. Ideally make it in advance and leave it to rest overnight so that the flavours can develop.

INGREDIENTS
SERVES 4

4 tbsp olive oil

1 large or 2 small onions, peeled and chopped finely

2 slim carrots, scrubbed and cut in rounds

2 sticks celery, chopped

4 large cloves garlic, peeled and sliced thinly

100g/4 oz green lentils

3 large bay leaves

1 x 400g/14 oz can tomatoes, broken up

600ml/1 ¼ pints/2 ½ cups gluten-free vegetable stock

400ml/14fl oz/1 ¾ cups full bodied red wine

6 gluten free vegan sausages, halved

1 x 400g/14 oz can borlotti beans, with their liquid

1 x 400g/14 oz can cannellini beans/white kidney beans, with their liquid

sea salt and freshly ground black pepper

METHOD

Heat the oil in a heavy casserole and add the onion, carrot, celery, and garlic.

Cook gently for 10–15 minutes until the vegetables are starting to soften but do not let them burn.

Add the lentils and bay leaves and continue to cook for a minute, stirring well.

Add the tomatoes and approximately half of the stock and wine.

Bring to the boil and simmer, uncovered for 35 minutes or until the lentils are nearly cooked, adding the extra liquid as it gets absorbed.

Add the sausages and cook for another few minutes.

Drain the beans but reserve their liquid.

Add the beans to the pot with enough of their liquid to make a thick sauce.

Season to taste and continue to simmer for a further 10 minutes to allow the flavour of the beans to integrate with the dish.

Ideally, allow the bean pot to cool and set aside for a few hours or overnight before reheating to serve. Serve with a green vegetable or salad.

KATHERINE'S CABBAGE WITH CHICKPEAS AND TAHINI DRESSING

The nutty richness of the tahini works really well with the crunch and slight bitterness of the cabbage.

INGREDIENTS
SERVES 2 GENEROUSLY AS A MAIN DISH OR 4 AS A SIDE DISH

1 tsp rice vinegar

3 tsp wheat/gluten-free tamari

1 tsp English mustard powder (check its ingredients to see it's gluten-free)

1 tbsp tahini

3 tbsp water

1 large red onion

1 large Savoy (or other) cabbage

1 tbsp oil

1 x 400g/14 oz can chickpeas, drained

METHOD

Put the rice vinegar, tamari, mustard, tahini, and water into a jar with a lid, tighten the lid and shake until mixed – or mix all the ingredients in a bowl with a whisk.

Leave at room temperature.

Cut the onion in half, remove the core and slice thinly.

Cut the cabbage into quarters, remove the core and slice thinly.

Heat the oil in a wok or large saucepan.

Add the cabbage and onions and cook for about 4–5 minutes, just to take the rawness off them.

Add the chickpeas and heat through for another couple of minutes.

Pour the dressing over and stir through thoroughly.

Serve immediately.

SWEDE/RUTABAGA AND CHICKPEA MUSH

This is super simple but really tasty. It makes a good dish on its own or a really filing accompaniment on a cold night with a couple of juicy vegan sausages or a burger.

INGREDIENTS
SERVES 4

3 tbsp olive oil

400g/14 oz swede/rutabaga, peeled and grated (shredded)

2 medium leeks, trimmed and sliced thinly

400g/14 oz can chickpeas, drained

200g/8 oz fresh spinach, washed and trimmed

sea salt and freshly ground black pepper

METHOD

Heat the oil in a heavy pan and add the swede/rutabaga and leeks.

Fry gently for a couple of minutes then cover the pan, turn down the heat and sweat for 30–40 minutes or until the vegetables are well cooked.

Add the chickpeas and the spinach and mix in well.

Continue to cook for a few minutes to allow the spinach to wilt then season to taste with sea salt and freshly ground black pepper.

FLAGEOLET, FENNEL AND CHARD ONE POT MEAL WITH GREEN PEPPERCORNS

A great one pot meal — vegetables included! If you are feeling energetic you can use dried beans and cook them overnight. The flavour and texture will be slightly better but there is so much going on in this dish that, realistically, you can get away with using canned beans.

INGREDIENTS
SERVES 4

250g/10 oz dried flageolet beans — or 3 x 400g/14 oz cans flageolet beans

1 heaped tbsp coconut oil or 2 tbsp olive oil

12 shallots, peeled

4 large cloves garlic, peeled and halved

2 sticks celery, finely chopped

8 pieces of okra, trimmed and sliced into rings

50g/2 oz piece of stem ginger, peeled and sliced finely

2 largish bulbs of fennel, trimmed and quartered

500ml/18fl oz/2 cups strong rice-based miso or gluten and wheat free vegetable stock

250ml/9fl oz/1 cup red wine

4 bay leaves

2 tsp black peppercorns

250g/10 oz rainbow chard

2 tsp green peppercorns

sea salt

METHOD

If you are using dried beans, soak them overnight, then drain and boil in plenty of fresh water for 1–1½ hours or until they are softening but not mushy. Drain.

Heat the coconut or olive oil in a heavy casserole and add the shallots, garlic, celery, okra, and ginger. Fry very gently for 10 minutes then add the quartered fennel bulbs and continue to sweat, covered for a further 10 minutes.

Add the dried cooked beans, miso and wine with the bay leaves and black peppercorns. Bring to the boil, cover, and simmer for a further 30 minutes or until the fennel and beans are cooked.

NB. If you are using canned beans, cook the fennel for 15 minutes with the miso and wine, then add the drained beans and continue to cook for another 15 minutes.

Chop the rainbow chard roughly, including the stems. Add it to the pot along with the green peppercorns. Cook for a further 5 minutes just to cook the chard, then season to taste with salt and serve.

PUY LENTILS WITH OKRA AND CORIANDER/CILANTRO

I have many variations of this basic recipe, christened by one lover of the dish, as my 'ploughed field' lentils! So, feel free to adapt it as you feel inclined. If you are unable to get the dark crunchy Puy lentils the dish will still work well with the more common green lentils. Like most such dishes it will taste better if you make it the day before you want to use it and let it rest overnight for the flavours to mature. The lentils should be served at room temperature so be sure you take them out of the fridge at least an hour before you want to serve them.

INGREDIENTS
SERVES 4

2 tbsp olive oil

1 large onion, peeled and chopped quite finely

3–4 large cloves garlic, peeled and finely sliced

2 small red chillies, deseeded and finely chopped

75g/3 oz okra, topped and sliced into rounds

300g/12 oz Puy lentils

4–6 bay leaves

750ml/1 ½ pints/3 cups gluten and wheat free vegetable stock

sea salt and freshly ground black pepper

juice 1–2 lemons

1–2 large handfuls of fresh coriander/cilantro, roughly chopped

METHOD

Heat the oil in a heavy pan and add the onions, garlic, chillies, and a pinch of salt to stop them burning. Fry gently for 5–10 minutes or until they are quite soft.

Add the okra, continue to fry for a minute or two longer then add the lentils and bay leaves.

Stir well to make sure they are well amalgamated then add the stock. Bring back to the boil, lower the heat and simmer, covered for 15 minutes.

Uncover and continue to simmer for a further 5–10 minutes or until the lentils are just cooked but still retain some texture and the liquid is virtually all absorbed. If they look as though they are drying out, add a little more liquid.

Season to taste with salt and freshly ground black pepper.

Leave to cool and rest, overnight if possible, to room temperature but do not chill (unless you want to store it).

Add lemon juice to taste and adjust the seasoning. Mix half the chopped coriander/cilantro into the dish and sprinkle the rest over the top to serve.

MUSHROOM AND TENDER STEM BROCCOLI WITH PUY LENTILS

A colourful and tasty combination. If you cannot find the dark and spicy Puy lentils, use dark green normal lentils.

You can use any variety of mushrooms that you fancy for this dish — from standard button or Portobello to more exotic chanterelles, oyster mushrooms, enoki or shitake, or a combination of several varieties.

You can serve the dish alone or with another green vegetable or salad.

INGREDIENTS
SERVES 4

4 large cloves garlic, peeled and finely chopped

8 tbsp olive oil

200g/8 oz Puy lentils

1 litre/2 ¼ pints/4 cups gluten-free vegetable stock

800ml/1 ¾ pints /3 ¼ cups red wine

450g/1 lb 2 oz tender stem broccoli

400g/1 lb fresh mushrooms — see above — roughly chopped

sea salt and freshly ground black pepper

METHOD

In a heavy bottomed pan gently sauté the garlic in 2 tablespoons of the olive oil until they are starting to soften.

Add the lentils, stir well and then add $^1/_3$ of the stock and wine. Simmer briskly, stirring regularly and adding more liquid as it is absorbed, for around 20 minutes or until the lentils are softened but still have good texture.

Season to taste with sea salt and freshly ground black pepper.

While the lentils are cooking, trim the stalks from the tender stem broccoli, chop them into 2 cm/½-inch lengths and steam for 5 minutes or until they are starting to soften. Add the florets and continue to steam for another 2–3 minutes or until the florets are slightly softened but still al dente.

Meanwhile, heat the remaining oil in a wide pan and briskly fry the chopped mushrooms for 2–3 minutes or until they are giving their juices and have softened.

In a warmed serving bowl, gently mix the lentils, with the broccoli and the mushrooms and their juices. Grind over a little extra black pepper and serve at once.

RICE & GRAIN BASED DISHES

Black rice pilaf with chard and lemon grass

Hot and spicy tofu paella

Tomato and coriander/cilantro risotto

Quinoa, mangetout/snow pea and roasted cashew nut salad

Anna's tomatoes stuffed with rice and potatoes

Broccoli with red rice and water chestnuts

Anna's risotto with asparagus

Roasted buckwheat (or kasha) with leeks, courgettes/zucchini and hazelnuts

Cabbage wrapped rice cake

Dried lime and mushroom pilaf

Once upon a time, the only rice that any of us knew was Uncle Ben's but today the rice possibilities are almost endless. Short or long grain, whole grain or polished, jasmine, basmati, Arborio risotto rice, sticky rice, red rice from the Camargue or forbidden black rice. Many rice have distinct flavours of their own, so it is nice to be able to build recipes around them.

Most of these dishes can be eaten warm or at room temperature and the flavours often develop if they are cooked at least a few hours before you want to eat them.

BLACK RICE PILAF WITH CHARD AND LEMON GRASS

Black rice (not to be confused with wild rice) is rather an exotic rice, much valued in ancient China where it was reserved for use by the aristocracy. It is slightly chewier that the more common paler varieties, but very tasty and it works really well with the smoky flavour of the smoked tofu.

INGREDIENTS
SERVES 4

2 level tbsp coconut oil

6 large spring onions, trimmed and cut in 2 cm/1in, lengths

4 large cloves garlic, peeled and sliced thinly

3–4 small hot red chillies, deseeded and cut into very small pieces

250g/10 oz black rice

1 level tbsp poppy seeds

250g/10 oz gluten-free smoked tofu cut into small dice

2 pieces lemon grass, course outer leaves discarded and cut into chunks

1 litre 500ml/3 pints/6 ¼ cups gluten-free miso

2 tbsp mirin

350g/14 oz fresh chard including stalks, washed

METHOD

Heat the oil in a wide pan and add the spring onions, garlic, and chillies. Cook gently for 8–10 minutes or until the garlic has softened. Do not burn.

Add the rice and stir around in the oil for a few minutes until it is well coated.

Add the poppy seeds, tofu, and lemon grass, $^2/_3$ of the miso and the mirin.

Bring to the boil and simmer fairly briskly for 40 minutes, or until the rice is coked but still slightly chewy, adding extra liquid as it is needed.

Cut the chard stalks into 2cm/1-inch pieces, and chop the leaves roughly.

After about 30 minutes, add the chard stalks and then, just before the rice is cooked, add the chard leaves. Stir in well and allow to wilt into the rice.

Check the seasoning, although you probably will not need any extra, and serve warm with a green salad.

HOT AND SPICY TOFU PAELLA

A classic paella is heavy with chicken pieces and mussels but in my vegan version I have substituted tofu for the chicken and tasty black olives for the mussels. What's not to like about that? With a good kick of chilli, it is perfect for that sunny weekend brunch.

Traditionally, a paella is served with chopped parsley, but I rather like it topped with chopped fresh coriander/cilantro.

INGREDIENTS
SERVES 4

2 generous pinches of saffron soaked in 3 tbsp of just-under-boiling water for 15 minutes

4 tbsp olive oil

2 level tsp paprika

1 large/2 small onions, peeled and finely chopped

2 large cloves of garlic, peeled and finely chopped

2 small hot red chillies, deseeded and finely chopped

1 large red bell pepper, deseeded and sliced thinly

200g/8 oz Spanish or other short grain rice, unwashed

300g/12 oz plain tofu, cut into 2cm/1 in cubes

1 x 400g/14 oz can chopped tomatoes

300ml/10fl oz/1 ¼ cups dry white wine

400ml/14fl oz//1 ¾ cups water

20–30 black olives, de-stoned and, depending on size halved

4 heaped tbsp frozen petits pois

generous handful of flat-leaf parsley or fresh coriander/cilantro, roughly chopped

1–2 lemons, quartered (optional)

sea salt and freshly ground black pepper

METHOD

Soak the saffron threads in the hot water.

Heat the oil in a large flat pan, skillet, or paella pan if you have one and add the paprika.

Stir around for a minute and then add the onion, garlic, chilli, and red pepper.

Stir well and fry gently for 10–15 minutes or until the peppers have started to soften.

Add the rice, stir well, and continue to cook for a minute

Add the tofu, the tomatoes, the saffron with its soaking water, the wine, and the water.

Season lightly and mix well.

Bring to the boil and then reduce the heat to a fairly brisk simmer and cook for 50–60 minutes, uncovered. You want the rice to be cooked but not mushy and still have some bite, and the liquid to be all but absorbed. If it is drying up too quickly add a little extra water. Traditionally you should not stir a paella while it is cooking, but I have done so without any dire results.

About 10 minutes before the rice is cooked, add the olives.

When the rice is cooked, adjust the seasoning to taste and then add the peas. You really only want them to defrost in the paella so that they retain both a slight crunch and their bright green colour.

Sprinkle generously with chopped parsley or coriander/cilantro and serve from the pan with lemon wedges for those who wish to add it.

TOMATO AND CORIANDER/ CILANTRO RISOTTO

INGREDIENTS
SERVES 4 GENEROUSLY

4 tbsp olive oil

4 heaped tsp paprika

1 medium large onion, peeled and chopped finely

2 large cloves of garlic, peeled and sliced thinly

2 large sticks celery, finely chopped

1 red pepper, deseeded and finely sliced

2 heaped tbsp tomato paste

2 large tomatoes, finely chopped

200g/8 oz risotto rice

750ml/1 ½ pints/3 cups hot, gluten-free vegetable stock

125ml/4fl oz/½ cup dry white wine

30 black olives, pitted and halved

2 large handfuls of fresh coriander/cilantro, roughly chopped

sea salt and freshly ground black pepper

METHOD

Heat the oil in a wide, flat pan and add the paprika. Stir for a minute. Add the onion, garlic, celery and pepper and sauté gently for 8–10 minutes or until the peppers are softening.

Stir in the tomato paste and the chopped tomatoes, stir and then add the rice.

Stir for two minutes and start adding the hot stock along with the white wine.

Simmer briskly, adding more liquid as it gets absorbed, for around 20–25 minutes or until the rice is cooked and the liquid has almost been absorbed. Add extra liquid of you need to. The end result should be moist, not dry like a pilau.

About 10 minutes before it is cooked, add the black olives. Season to taste.

Serve heavily sprinkled with chopped fresh coriander/cilantro.

QUINOA, MANGETOUT/SNOW PEA AND ROASTED CASHEW NUT SALAD

The fresh green crispness of the mangetouts/snow peas contrasts well with chewier textures of the nuts and the quinoa and is given a welcome touch of sharpness by the lemon juice. A lovely summer lunch dish.

INGREDIENTS
SERVES 4

3 tbsp olive oil

6-8 large spring onions/scallions

2 tsp crushed coriander seeds

200g /8 oz quinoa grains

750ml/1 ½ pints/3 cups gluten-free vegetable stock

100g/4 oz fresh baby spinach leaves

100g/4 oz mangetout/snow peas cut in halves or thirds

75g/3 oz roast, salted cashew nuts

juice 1 lemon

handful of fresh coriander leaves

sea salt and freshly ground black pepper

METHOD

Heat the oil in a wide pan and add the spring onions/scallions and coriander seeds.

Fry gently for 2–3 minutes then add the quinoa and stock. Bring to the boil then lower the heat and simmer for 15 minutes.

Add the spinach and continue to cook for a further 10 minutes or until the quinoa is cooked. Add extra liquid if needed.

Meanwhile, steam the mangetouts/snow peas for no more than a couple of minutes — to slightly take the edge off their rawness. You want them to stay both crisp and very green so do not overcook. Immediately plunge into cold water.

Add the mangetouts/snow peas with the cashew nuts to the quinoa and mix well.

Season to taste (you should need very little salt) and add the lemon. Chop the coriander and sprinkle it generously over the dish. Serve at room temperature.

ANNA'S TOMATOES STUFFED WITH RICE AND POTATOES

This is one of Anna's favourite, simplest and most delicious dishes. It appeared in our *'Simply Italian, Simply Gluten Free'* book last year, but I could not resist including it here as well.

INGREDIENTS
SERVES 4

4 large, ripe but firm tomatoes, such as beef tomatoes, each weighing about 200g/8 oz

a pinch of chilli flakes

50g/2 oz uncooked Italian risotto rice (eg Arborio, Carnaroli, Vialone Nano)

4 tbsp olive oil (with extra for greasing the dish)

1 small garlic clove, chopped

8 black olives, pitted and chopped fairly small

1 tbsp flat-leaf parsley, chopped

1 level tbsp tomato purée

2 medium potatoes, cut into very small cubes

2 tsp dried oregano

sea salt and freshly ground black pepper

METHOD

Heat the oven to 180°C/350°F/Gas Mark 4.

Cut the top off each tomato and reserve. Scoop the flesh and seeds out of the tomatoes, discard some of the seeds. Chop the flesh into small pieces and place it in a bowl with a pinch of salt and the chilli flakes.

Add the rice, 3 tablespoons of the olive oil, the garlic, olives, parsley, and tomato purée. Mix thoroughly.

Taste and adjust the seasoning to your liking.

Sprinkle the inside of the tomatoes with salt and fill them with the mixture. Lid them with the reserved tomato tops.

Put the tomatoes in an oiled overproof dish into which they will fit comfortably but not too loosely.

Put the cubed potatoes in a bowl, spoon over 1 tablespoon of the remaining olive oil and mix well to coat all the cubes, then arrange them around the tomatoes in the dish.

Shower the tomatoes with the remaining oil and the oregano.

Cook for 1 hour 30 minutes or until the potatoes and rice are both cooked. Serve at once with a salad.

BROCCOLI WITH RED RICE AND WATER CHESTNUTS

The chewiness of the red rice contrasts well with the crunchiness of the water chestnuts and the slightly softer broccoli.

INGREDIENTS
SERVES 4

2 tbsp olive oil

2 medium onions, finely chopped

200g/8 oz brown or red Camargue rice

approx. 1 litre 400ml/3 pints/6 cups gluten/wheat-free vegetable stock

400g/14 oz small fresh broccoli florets

1 x 225g/8 oz can water chestnuts, drained, and sliced

2 heaped tbsp gluten-free wholegrain mustard

2 heaped tbsp soya or coconut yogurt

sea salt and freshly ground black pepper

METHOD

Heat the oil and gently cook the onions till they soften.

Add the rice and 2/3 of the stock.

Bring to the boil and simmer briskly for 30–40 minutes, adding the extra liquid as it is absorbed, or until the rice pleasantly chewy but not soft.

Blanch the broccoli florets for 3–4 minutes in boiling water until starting to soften but still slightly crunchy.

Drain the water chestnuts, slice in half.

Mix the mustard with the yogurt and mix into the rice and season to taste with salt and pepper.

Add the water chestnuts and the broccoli and mix all gently together. Serve at once.

ANNA'S RISOTTO WITH ASPARAGUS

This recipe of Anna's is one of my favourites. She maintains that classic Italian risottos should always be made with butter but if you are vegan or on a milk-free diet, it seems a shame to deprive yourself of this treat — and I think it works very well with olive oil.

INGREDIENTS
SERVES 4

350g/14 oz asparagus

2 litres/4 pints /8 ½ cups gluten free vegetable stock

3 tbsp light olive oil

2 shallots, finely chopped

350g/12 oz Italian risotto rice (eg Arborio, Carnaroli, Vialone Nano)

2 tbsp white vermouth

100g/4 oz freshly vegan hard cheese (optional)

sea salt and freshly ground black pepper

METHOD

Wash and trim the asparagus, cut off the hard ends of the stalks and put in a saucepan with the stock. Bring to the boil and boil for 15 minutes. (NB: You are cooking the hard stalks in the stock to give it flavour; you will not be using them in the dish.)

Scoop out and discard the stalks and keep the stock simmering for the whole of the cooking time since you must add simmering liquid to the rice for a risotto.

Cut the tender part of the asparagus into roughly 2 cm/1-inch pieces, and set aside the spear tops.

Heat half the olive oil, add the shallots and sauté gently until soft.

Add the asparagus pieces but not the spears. Sauté gently for 5 minutes, stirring constantly, then add the rice.

Continue cooking until the rice grains appear translucent and well coated with the oil.

Splash with the vermouth, cook for a minute or two and then begin to add the stock, one ladleful at a time. When the rice looks dry add another ladleful and then another, until the rice is cooked. If you have finished all the stock and the rice is not cooked to your liking, just add extra boiling water.

About 5 minutes before the rice in ready (good Italian rice takes about 18–20 minutes to cook depending on the variety) add the asparagus spears and salt and pepper to taste.

When the rice in done, turn off the heat, add the remaining oil, cover the pan, and allow it to rest for 2 minutes.

Stir energetically and bring to the table. You can serve it with some grated vegan hard cheese or just with freshly ground black pepper.

ROASTED BUCKWHEAT GROATS (OR KASHA) WITH LEEKS, COURGETTES/ZUCCHINI AND HAZELNUTS

Roasting buckwheat groats gives them a delicious nutty flavour which is complemented by the roast hazelnuts in this recipe. Kasha is already roasted so if you can find it, you'll save yourself the trouble of roasting. Be careful not to overcook the buckwheat – you want it to keep its texture, not turn to mush! The raw grated courgettes/zucchini add an extra layer of texture. If you cannot eat nuts, try roasted pumpkin seeds as a more than satisfactory alternative for the hazelnuts.

INGREDIENTS
SERVES 4

2 tbsp olive oil

4 leeks, thinly sliced

200g/8oz roasted buckwheat groats/kasha

500ml/18fl oz/2 cups gluten and wheat free vegetable stock

2 large courgettes/zucchini, coarsely grated

100g/4 oz toasted hazelnuts, roughly chopped or if you cannot eat nuts, roasted pumpkin seeds

sea salt and freshly ground black pepper

METHOD

Heat the oil in a medium saucepan or a deep, frying pan and gently cook the leeks for at least 10 minutes until they are soft, stirring frequently to prevent burning.

Meanwhile, in a small pan with a lid, bring the stock to a boil. Turn the heat right down and stir in the buckwheat/kasha.

Cover the pan and cook for 6–8 minutes, stirring once or twice but being sure not to overcook. Turn off the heat but leave the pan covered.

Once the leeks are cooked, stir in the buckwheat/kasha, courgettes/ zucchini and hazelnuts or pumpkin seeds.

Season to taste before serving.

CABBAGE WRAPPED RICE CAKE

Another of the dishes that Katherine created for the *FoodsMatter* newsletter. She suggests sprinkling some flaked almonds or seeds over the top of the rice cake for the final 10 minutes of cooking to add some colour and a tasty crunch.

INGREDIENTS
SERVES 4

8–10 large cabbage leaves

100g/4 oz short grain brown rice

1 tbsp olive oil

1 medium onion, finely chopped

1 level tsp dried thyme

1 level tsp dried oregano

1 level tsp dried mint

250g/10 oz plain tofu, crumbled

80g/3 oz black olives, pitted and halved

80g/3 oz pine nuts, lightly toasted in a dry frying pan

2 medium size tomatoes, chopped small

1 courgette/zucchini, grated

zest of 1 lemon

sea salt and freshly ground black pepper

handful of flaked almonds or 1 tbsp sesame seeds (optional)

METHOD

Wash the cabbage leaves, cut out the hard bit of the stem and steam for 5 minutes until the leaves have softened.

Drain on a tea towel to remove excess water.

Meanwhile cook the rice in plenty of fast boiling water or gluten-free vegetable stock for 8–10 minutes or until it is just cooked but not mushy. Drain and set aside

Heat the oven to 180°C/350°/F/Gas mark 4.

Heat the oil in a frying pan and gently cook the onion and herbs until the onion is soft.

Crumble in the tofu then stir in the rice with the olives, pine nuts, chopped tomato, courgette/zucchini, and lemon zest. Mix gently but thoroughly.

Grease a 20 cm/8-inch spring form cake tin/pan, and line with the cabbage leaves making sure that the leaves that line the sides hang over the top of the tin/pan so that they can wrap over the top of the rice.

Fill the tin/pan with the rice mixture and pat down firmly with a spoon.

Fold over the leaves from the sides so they cover the top.

Place on a baking sheet and bake for 20 minutes.

Remove the sides of the tin/pan and carefully turn the cake upside down onto the baking sheet.

Remove the bottom section of the tin, sprinkle with flaked almonds or sesame seeds if you are using them and return to the oven for another 15 minutes.

Serve with a green salad.

DRIED LIME AND MUSHROOM PILAF

Dried limes are a staple in Arabic cookery and give a subtle, pleasantly bitter undertone to a dish. You should be able to buy them in any Middle Eastern supermarket or online.

INGREDIENTS
SERVES 4

6 tbsp olive oil

2 level tsp cumin

1 large onion, peeled and sliced thinly

4 cloves garlic, peeled and sliced thinly

2 sticks celery, chopped roughly

75g/3 oz okra, topped and tailed and sliced in thin rounds

½ a medium aubergine, diced fairly small

150g/6 oz wholegrain rice

3 dried limes (from any Middle Eastern grocery store, or online), pierced a couple of times with a knife or skewer

500ml/18fl oz/2 cups gluten/wheat-free vegetable stock

100g/4 oz fresh leaf spinach, washed and roughly chopped

juice 1–2 lemons

sea salt and fresh ground black pepper

150g/6 oz chestnut mushrooms, sliced

large handful parsley, chopped roughly

METHOD

Heat 4 tablespoons of oil in a wide pan and add the cumin, onion, 2 of the garlic cloves and the celery.

Fry together fairly briskly but without burning, for 4–5 minutes.

Add the okra and aubergine, mix well then lower the heat, cover the pan, and sweat for 15 minutes or until all the vegetables are soft.

Add the rice, stir well, then add the pierced limes and stock.

Cover and simmer for 15–20 minutes or until the rice is nearly cooked and most of the liquid absorbed. Turn off the heat.

Add the spinach, stir it in, and allow to wilt in the heat of the dish then season with salt, pepper, and lemon juice to taste.

Meanwhile, heat the remaining oil in a separate pan and gently fry the remaining garlic for a couple of minutes.

Add the sliced mushrooms and fry briskly until they start to release their juices then stir into the rice mixture.

Just before you are ready to serve the dish, stir in the chopped parsley.

Serve at room temperature with a green salad.

SALADS

Warm salad of potatoes and green beans with pesto

Anna's cannellini/white kidney beans sautéed in garlic oil

Beetroot and carrot salad with horseradish

Baked onion and tomato salad

Grilled/broiled peppers with hummus

Katherine's crunchy Asian salad with quick chilli dressing

Fennel, green bean, avocado and mint salad

Courgettes/zucchini with okra, butter beans and pine nuts

Steamed fennel salad with radicchio

Salads these days are nearly always made with raw vegetables and fruit and served cold, but this was not always the case. You will find many of the recipes below use cooked vegetables and are served warm.

My approach to making raw salad is very similar to my approach to vegetable dishes. Buy up as many interesting ingredients as you can find and fit into your fridge and then use them in different combinations each day, enlivened with fresh herbs, handfuls of nuts or seeds and good dressings.

My fall back (actually, preferred) dressing is always sea salt, freshly ground pepper, lemon juice or cider vinegar and lots of good olive oil. But it can be fun to experiment with mayonnaise, horseradish, thousand island dressing, salsa or whatever you fancy. But... make sure that the dressing is not too thick and that you do not use too much of it. In either case you risk ending up with a claggy mess.

My other two golden rules for making salads:

Do not use too many ingredients or you will confuse their flavours.

With the exception of raw leek or onion, which do need to be sliced very thinly, do not cut your vegetables too small. Again, they will lose their flavour and texture and become a confused mess. You need to be able to taste each ingredient both separately and with its fellows.

WARM SALAD OF POTATOES AND GREEN BEANS WITH PESTO

I love 'warm' salads – not hot but not fridge cold either.

INGREDIENTS
SERVES 4

50g/2 oz fresh basil leaves

2 garlic cloves, peeled

25g/1 oz pine nuts

sea salt and freshly ground black pepper

5 tbsp extra virgin olive oil

750g/1lb 6 oz new potatoes, all the same size

450g/1lb French/green beans/fagiolini

METHOD

Make the pesto. These amounts will probably make more pesto that you need for this dish so can be used for another recipe — or just on gluten-free toast or as a dip. It will keep in the fridge for 2–3 days.

Put all the basil leaves, garlic, pine nuts, salt, pepper and 2 tablespoons of the olive oil into a food processor and whizz until completely blended. Taste and check the seasonings.

Boil the potatoes in their skins. When cooked, drain, and peel them while still hot. Leave them aside.

Top the beans and cook them in well salted water until tender but not soft — a sharp knife should go through them easily and they will still be a lovely green colour.

Drain and dry them and cut into 2.5 cm/1-inch lengths.

While the beans are cooking, cut the potatoes into 2 cm/¾-inch cubes, put them in a bowl and dress with the remaining olive oil.

Add the beans to the potatoes, spoon at least half the pesto into the salad and toss gently.

Add extra pesto if you think it needs it and serve warm.

ANNA'S CANNELLINI/WHITE KIDNEY BEANS SAUTÉED IN GARLIC OIL

As with so many of Anna's recipes, this is incredibly simple — but totally delicious. I have really lost count of how often I have looked at one of her recipes and thought: 'Surely it can't just be that?'... But it is — and it works. From Anna's book '*Simply Italian, Simply Gluten Free*'.

INGREDIENTS
SERVES 4

3 garlic cloves

4 tbsp extra virgin oil

12 sage leaves, coarsely torn

1–2 pinches chilli flakes

2 x 400g/14oz cans cannellini/white kidney beans

sea salt

METHOD

Chop the garlic cloves. If the garlic is old, cut the cloves in half and remove the germ before chopping — this will make the garlic sweeter.

Put the garlic in the frying pan with the oil, sage and chilli and fry gently until it begins to colour.

Drain and rinse the cannellini/white kidney beans and add to the frying pan

Mix well and cook over a low heat for 5 minutes. Stirring frequently.

Taste, add salt if necessary and serve.

BEETROOT AND CARROT SALAD WITH HORSERADISH

A really bright and colourful salad — given a wonderful edge by the horseradish. If you can find a horseradish root, you can used pre-grated fresh horseradish; if you can't find either, you can buy horseradish sauce in a jar which will do just as well.

INGREDIENTS
SERVES 4

3 small fresh beetroots, scrubbed and grated coarsely

2 medium carrots, scrubbed and grated coarsely

3-6 heaped tsp grated horseradish, depending on how hot you want your salad

juice 1 large lemon

½ tsp sea salt

½ tsp fresh ground black pepper

2-3 tbsp olive oil

large bunch fresh coriander/cilantro leaves, washed

METHOD

In a bowl, mix the grated beetroots and carrots well together.

In a separate bowl mix the horseradish with the lemon juice, salt, pepper, and oil to make the dressing. If it is too thick, dilute with a little boiling water.

Mix the dressing thoroughly into the salad and turn into a serving bowl.

Scatter a thick layer of chopped coriander/cliantro leaves over the salad before serving

BAKED ONION AND TOMATO SALAD

Cooking the onions very slowly with the tomatoes gives a lovely depth of flavour. A delicious side salad — or even something rather tasty to nibble with a drink.

INGREDIENTS
SERVES 4

20 very small onions or shallots, peeled but left whole

4 cloves garlic, peeled and left whole

12 baby plum or cherry tomatoes

4 tbsp olive oil

METHOD

Peel the onions and garlic and put in a heavy, shallow lidded pan with the oil and tomatoes.

Heat gradually, cover the pan and cook very gently for 30–45 minutes or until the onions are quite soft and the juices slightly caramelised.

You can season if you want to, but I don't think it needs salt or pepper.

Serve at room temperature.

STEAMED FENNEL SALAD WITH RADICCHIO

So simple – but really tasty. But make sure not to overcook the fennel.

INGREDIENTS
SERVES 4

2 large or 4 small heads of fennel

1–2 heads radicchio, depending on size

sea salt and freshly ground black pepper

2 tbsp cider vinegar

4 tbsp olive oil

METHOD

Halve or quarter the fennel, depending on size, and steam for 8–10 minutes or until they are soft without being mushy.

Turn into a bowl.

Chop the radicchio roughly and mix into the fennel.

Dress to taste with salt, pepper, cider vinegar and oil and serve at room temperature.

GRILLED/BROILED PEPPERS WITH HUMMUS

A really simple but colourful and tasty lunch dish.

INGREDIENTS
SERVES 4

4 largish bell peppers – different colours

12–15 baby plum or cherry tomatoes

olive oil

Herbes de Provence or other dried mixed herbs

sea salt and freshly ground black pepper

approx. 350g/12 oz homemade or bought hummus (be sure to check the ingredients)

small bunch fresh chives

METHOD

Halve the peppers and remove the seeds.

Halve the tomatoes.

Lay the peppers skin side up on a grill/broiler pan covered in foil. Drizzle with olive oil and grill/broil until the skin is blistered and blackened. Leave to cool and peel off the skin.

Return the peppers to the grill/broiler pan, cut side up and fill each with the halved tomatoes, also cut side up.

Sprinkle with the dried herbs, sea salt and black pepper.

Grill/broil until the tomatoes are softening slightly but not falling apart — 4–6 minutes depending on the tomatoes.

Remove from the grill/broiler, cool slightly and then cover each pepper and tomato with a good blob of hummus.

Sprinkle with chopped chives and serve as a starter or a light salad for lunch.

KATHERINE'S CRUNCHY ASIAN SALAD WITH QUICK CHILLI DRESSING

This salad is loosely based on coleslaw but made with vegetables you might expect to find in a stir fry. The seeds are optional, but they do give a lovely dry savoury note to the vegetables.

INGREDIENTS
SERVES 4

½ Chinese leaf cabbage, finely sliced

6 spring onions/scallions, finely sliced

large handful of bean sprouts

2 medium red or orange bell peppers, de-seeded and finely sliced

large handful of sunflower seeds

6 tbsp vegan/egg free mayonnaise

4 tbsp gluten-free chilli dipping sauce (check ingredients)

METHOD

Mix the Chinese leaf, spring onions/scallions, bean sprouts and peppers together in a large bowl.

Heat a dry frying pan and toast the sunflower seeds until they start to pop.

Stir them through the raw vegetables.

In a small bowl, thoroughly mix the mayonnaise and chilli sauce. If it is too thick, dilute with a little boiling water.

Mix the dressing well into the salad and serve.

FENNEL, GREEN BEAN, AVOCADO AND MINT SALAD

Delicious and filling. To make it nut free, substitute pumpkin seeds for the pecans, and sesame seeds for the ground hazelnuts.

INGREDIENTS
SERVES 4

1 x 400g/14 oz can of haricot/navy beans

200g/8 oz fine green beans

sea salt and freshly ground black pepper

2 tbsp olive oil

juice of 2–3 lemons

2 heads fennel

50g/2 oz fresh okra

1 large or 2 small ripe avocados

large handful of fresh mint

METHOD

Tip the haricot/navy beans into a pot and heat gently till well warmed but nowhere near boiling. Drain. (They absorb the dressing much better if they are warm.)

Meanwhile, trim the green beans and halve them, then steam for 2–3 minutes or until they are slightly softened but still crunchy.

Tip the haricot/navy beans and the green beans into a bowl and dress with salt, pepper olive oil and lemon juice. You will need extra lemon juice to toss the fennel and the avocado to stop them going brown.

Finely slice the fennel, toss in lemon juice, and then add to the beans. Top and tail the okra, slice quite thinly and add to the salad.

Peel the avocados, cut into largish dice, and toss in lemon juice the add to the salad

Chop the mint roughly and add to the salad and then toss all very gently so as not to crush the avocado. Dress with some fennel fronds if you have any left.

Serve at room temperature.

COURGETTES/ZUCCHINI WITH OKRA, BUTTER BEANS AND PINE NUTS

A simple dish that is great as either a starter or a lunch dish. Serve with gluten-free crackers or fresh gluten-free bread.

INGREDIENTS
SERVES 4

4 medium courgettes/zucchini, topped and tailed and sliced thinly lengthways

6–8 tbsp olive oil, and extra to oil griddle

dried Herbes de Provence or mixed herbs

4 large cloves garlic, peeled and sliced

200g/8 oz fresh okra, topped and tailed and sliced in thickish rounds

200g/8 oz button mushrooms, wiped, and halved if they are large

400g/14 oz can of butter beans, drained

50g/2 oz pine nuts

juice 1 lemon

sea salt and freshly ground black pepper

large handful of fresh coriander/cilantro, chopped

METHOD

Lightly oil a griddle or spread the courgettes/zucchini slices out on some foil on a grill/broiler pan. Sprinkle lightly with the herbs and griddle or broil on a medium high heat, until the slices are soft.

Transfer them onto a serving dish and spread them out across the dish to form a bed for the other vegetables.

Meanwhile, put three tablespoons of the oil into a wide frying pan and add the garlic slices and the okra.

Cook gently for 3–4 minutes then add the mushrooms.

Continue to cook relatively gently until the mushrooms start to give their juices, then add the butter beans. Turn the heat very low to allow the butter beans to heat through.

Dry fry the pine nuts (or toast them under a grill/broiler) making sure that they do not burn.

Add the pine nuts to the bean and okra mixture then season well with sea salt and freshly ground black pepper and dress with the lemon juice and the remaining oil.

Finally, when you are ready to serve the dish, stir in the chopped fresh coriander and spoon the mixture over the courgettes/zucchini slices on the dish.

DESSERTS

||||||||||||||||||||||||||||||||

Apple and ginger tart

Avocado and pineapple parfait

Chocolate avocado pots

Cranberry and pecan brûlée

Pears baked with ginger

Nutty greengage or damson crumble/crisp

Glorious gooseberry gunge

Strawberries with Pimm's and cashew cream

Hot mango and pineapple with rum and chilli

Katherine's chocolate mousse with cherries

Katherine's aubergine/eggplant rich chocolate mousse

Blood orange iced dessert

Coffee and Tia Maria ice cream

Banana, coconut milk and ginger ice cream

Katherine is a much keener dessert maker than I am, so I have included a few of her creations including two of her unusual chocolate mousses — one with aquafaba and one with aubergine.

In fact, there are several desserts made either with aubergine or avocado, both of which, being soft and smooth and neutral, rather than specifically savoury in flavour, work very well as bases for desserts.

I love fruit as a dessert as I find it such a refreshing way to end a meal. So, most of the other dessert recipes are based on, or at the very least, contain fruit — even the ice creams!

APPLE AND GINGER TART

This tart's cheesecake style base means it is quick and easy to make. Make sure that you have a really thick layer of apples on top. Because you are only using vegan spread or coconut oil to hold the biscuits together the base may be rather crumbly — but no less delicious.

You should be able to buy gluten-free vegan gingernut biscuits, but if not, vegan gluten-free digestive/graham crackers or oaty biscuits will do just as well. In which case, you might want to substitute half a teaspoon of ground cinnamon for the ginger.

INGREDIENTS
SERVES 4

100g/4 oz wheat, gluten and milk-free gingernut, digestives/ graham crackers or oaty biscuits/ cookies

2 or 3 eating apples

1 tbsp caster sugar

75g/3 oz vegan spread or coconut oil

1 level tsp ground ginger or, if you are using digestives or oaty biscuits/cookies, substitute with ½ tsp cinnamon

METHOD

Grease and line the base of a 20 cm/8-inch loose bottom round cake tin/pan.

Preheat the oven to 200°C/400°F/Gas Mark 6.

Put the biscuits/cookies in a bag or large bowl and crush to a fine, even crumb, with a rolling pin.

Melt 50g/2 oz of the spread/coconut oil and stir into the crumbs.

Press the crumb mixture into the base of the tin/pan.

Put the base in the fridge while you prepare the topping.

Peel and core the apples and cut into quarters.

Thinly slice the apples and then place around the edge of the tin/pan, overlapping the slices.

Repeat to fill the hole in the centre.

The apples in the centre of my tart stuck up quite a lot but they sank down during cooking.

Melt the remaining 25g/1 oz of spread/coconut oil and then stir in the sugar and ginger or cinnamon. Brush the mixture gently over the top of the apples.

Bake for about 35 minutes until the apples are a little brown at the edges.

Allow the tart to cool in the tin before serving with a vegan cream or ice cream.

AVOCADO AND PINEAPPLE PARFAIT

Avocado makes a deliciously smooth base for a dessert. The contrast with the sweet sharpness of the pineapples works really well.

INGREDIENTS
SERVES 4

2 ripe avocados, peeled and stone removed

3 thick slices fresh pineapple

grated zest and juice of 2 limes

1–2 tbsp agave syrup

seeds from ½ fresh pomegranate or 2 tbsp red currants

METHOD

Put all the ingredients except the pomegranate seeds or red currants into a liquidiser or food processor and whizz until you have a smooth mousse.

Stir in the seeds or redcurrants and transfer into glasses to serve.

CHOCOLATE AVOCADO POTS

If you want to give this dessert a little extra bite, finely chop 4-6 pieces of stem ginger and stir in at the end.

INGREDIENTS
SERVES 4

100g/4 oz, 85% cocoa solids vegan chocolate

2 ripe avocados, peeled and destoned

3 tbsp brandy

approx. 1 tbsp agave syrup — to taste

4–6 pieces stem ginger, finely chopped

extra grated chocolate, stem ginger pieces or a few fresh raspberries to decorate

METHOD

Melt the chocolate in a microwave, or in a bowl over barely simmering hot water. Allow to cool.

Put the avocado , chocolate, brandy and agave to taste in a food processor or liquidiser and purée. Stir in the ginger pieces if you are using them.

Spoon into small pots or glasses and decorate with chocolate, stem ginger or raspberries.

CRANBERRY AND PECAN BRÛLÉE

This recipe was devised as a way of using up excess cranberries after Christmas — but it works at any time of the year! The sharpness of the cranberries contrasts deliciously with the banana and the crunchy nuts on the top. You could also add a spoonful of coconut or soya vanilla ice cream to each as you serve it.

INGREDIENTS
SERVES 4

275g/11 oz fresh cranberries

2 medium bananas

grated zest and juice of 2 limes

4 tbsp Cointreau or Grand Marnier

approx 50g/2 oz halved pecans

1 tbsp caster/superfine sugar

soya or coconut vanilla ice cream

METHOD

In a food processor, roughly purée the cranberries, bananas, lime zest and juice with the liqueur.

You will need to decide how smooth or 'bitty' you wish it to be and process accordingly.

Spoon the mixture into six ovenproof ramekin dishes or small pots, arrange the pecans in a pattern on the top and sprinkle lightly with the sugar.

To serve, grill/broil under a hot grill/broiler for 3–4 minutes or until the sugar has melted and caramelised slightly.

Serve at once with a spoonful of vegan ice cream (optional).

PEARS BAKED WITH GINGER

The pears are delicious on their own, but you can also serve them with whatever kind of ginger ice cream you can eat. The recipes also works well with pine nuts as an alternative to walnuts.

INGREDIENTS
SERVES 4

4 ripe pears, cored with an apple corer

small to medium knob of fresh ginger (depending how keen you are on ginger), peeled and cut in very thin slices

2 tbsp broken walnuts nuts or pine nuts

2 tbsp raisins (optional)

approx 150ml/5fl oz/ 2/3 cup ginger wine

METHOD

Heat the oven to 180°C/350°F/Gas Mark 4.

Arrange the cored pears in an ovenproof baking dish.

Insert the ginger slithers mixed with the nuts and raisins if you are using them, down the central hole in the pears, sprinkling any extra around the fruit in the dish.

Pour around the ginger wine — it should be about 2 cm/1-inch deep — then cover the pears with aluminium foil and bake for 30–40 minutes depending on how ripe they are.

Serve warm with the extra juice and nuts.

NUTTY GREENGAGE, DAMSON OR ANY SOFT FRUIT CRUMBLE/CRISP

You can use this mixture for plums, blackberries and apples or any other combination of seasonal fruits, although you may want to adjust the amount of sugar according to the tartness of the fruit. If you cannot find pecan nuts, you can substitute broken walnuts.

INGREDIENTS
SERVES 6

700g/1lb 5 oz greengage or damson plums

2 tbsp agave or maple syrup or light muscovado/raw sugar

60ml /2fl oz/¼ cup water

75g/3 oz gluten-free porridge or rolled oats

50g/2 oz ground almonds

20g /½ oz flaked almonds

50g/2 oz pecan nuts

25g/1 oz demerara/dark brown sugar

METHOD

Heat the oven to 180°C/350°F/Gas Mark 4.

Lay out the greengages or damsons in bottom of an ovenproof pie dish/pan and spoon over the agave or maple syrup or the sugar.

Add the water.

In a bowl, mix the oats with ground almonds, flaked almonds, pecan nuts and sugar then spread this mixture over the fruit.

Bake, uncovered, for 40 minutes and serve warm or at room temperature on its own or with vegan cream, yogurt, or ice cream.

GLORIOUS GOOSEBERRY GUNGE

This recipe started off as an egg-free cake recipe, but although the flavour is delicious, the texture really did not work — so, I reduced the amount of flour and turned it into this really yummy gungy gooseberry pudding. Even gunge-ier and better when eaten with a free-from ice cream or yogurt.

You can, of course, make a similar glorious gunge with any other soft fruit in season.

INGREDIENTS
SERVES 4

275g/10 oz fresh gooseberries, topped and tailed

1 generous tbsp agave syrup or fruit sugar

juice ½ large lemon

50g/2 oz green raisins (they do not have to be green but match the colour of the gooseberries better if they are!)

50g/2 oz self-raising gluten and wheat-free flour

2 level tsp gluten and wheat-free baking powder

METHOD

Heat the oven to 180°C/350°F/Gas Mark 4.

Whizz the raw gooseberries, briefly, in a food processor with the agave syrup or fruit syrup and the lemon juice — you want them to remain quite lumpy so only whiz for a matter of seconds.

Turn into a bowl, stir in the raisins then fold in the flour with the baking powder.

Spoon into an oven-proof baking dish and bake for 30 minutes.

Serve warm with vegan cream, ice cream or yogurt of your choice.

STRAWBERRIES WITH PIMM'S AND CASHEW CREAM

A really pretty dessert best served in a glass or jar.

INGREDIENTS
SERVES 4

200g/8 oz cashew nuts

zest of 1 orange

400g/16 oz fresh ripe strawberries

60ml/2fl oz/¼ cup Pimm's

1 tbsp caster/superfine sugar

50g/2 oz gluten-free oats

50g/2 oz brown sugar

METHOD

Place the cashew nuts in a bowl and cover with water and leave to soak for at least an hour to soften.

Drain the cashews and blend in a liquidiser, slowly adding water until you have the consistency of double cream.

Stir in the orange zest and chill until needed.

Hull the strawberries and chop each one into about 8 pieces.

Place in a bowl and pour over the Pimm's and caster/superfine sugar and leave to soak for 30 minutes.

Place the oats and brown sugar in a small flat pan.

Cook over a low heat and stir continuously until you have crunchy crumbs then spread out on a plate to cool.

When you are ready to serve, mix the oats into the cashew cream.

Place a layer of strawberries into the bottom of 4 glasses then spoon some cashew cream on top of the strawberries.

Repeat with another layer of strawberries and cream and serve immediately.

HOT MANGO AND PINEAPPLE WITH RUM AND CHILLI

Hot fruit salads seem a bit counterintuitive but actually, are delicious. And this one is hot in every sense. It is great served with coconut yogurt or vegan ice cream.

INGREDIENTS
SERVES 4

1 large or 2 small mangoes, peeled and cut into 1–2cm/ ½ –1-inch pieces

½ pineapple, peeled and cut into similar size pieces

1–2 small hot red chillies (depending on how fiery you like), deseeded and finely chopped

1 heaped tbsp brown sugar

6 tbsp rum

juice of 2 limes

lime zest to serve (optional)

coconut or soya yogurt or ice cream

METHOD

Heat the oven to 180°C/350°F/Gas Mark 4.

Place the mango and pineapple chunks into an ovenproof dish.

Sprinkle over the chilli and sugar.

Pour over the rum and lime juice.

Cover lightly and bake for 20 minutes.

Sprinkle over the lime zest if using it and serve alone or with yogurt or ice cream.

KATHERINE'S CHOCOLATE MOUSSE WITH CHERRIES

The structure of this mousse comes from the liquid in a can of chickpeas. Known as aquafaba, it has many of the qualities of egg whites when whisked. It even has its own Facebook group who share the results of experimenting with it!

INGREDIENTS
SERVES 4

1 can of cherries in syrup

200g /8 oz dairy free dark chocolate

aquafaba liquid drained from 1 x 400g/14 oz can of chickpeas

20-25g/¾ -1oz caster sugar/superfine sugar

METHOD

Heat the cherries and their syrup, over a low heat while you prepare the mousse. You are looking for the cherries to soften and the liquid to reduce.

Let them cool a little before you put the mousse on top.

Gently melt the chocolate either on a low setting in the microwave or in a bowl resting above a pan of barely simmering water.

Once it has melted, set aside to cool.

Meanwhile, in a large bowl whisk the aquafaba mixture until you have soft peaks.

Add the sugar and whisk again until you have stiffish peaks.

Fold the chocolate into the aquafaba very gently with a metal spoon.

Divide the cherries between four glasses, straining a little as you do if there is a lot of liquid left.

Carefully spoon the chocolate mousse over the top of the cherries and place in the fridge to set.

KATHERINE'S AUBERGINE/EGGPLANT RICH CHOCOLATE MOUSSE

This is not as light and fluffy as an egg-based mousse, but its rich chocolatey-ness makes it even more delicious.

INGREDIENTS
SERVES 4

1 medium aubergine/eggplant

200g /8 oz dark/bittersweet dairy-free chocolate

2 tbsp agave syrup or fruit sugar

16 tbsp oat, soya, or coconut cream

handful of raisins, chopped prunes or dairy-free chocolate chips — optional

1 tbsp chopped toasted nuts or seeds to decorate

METHOD
Pierce the aubergine/eggplant skin a few times and cook until it is really soft. It takes about 8 minutes in the microwave in a covered bowl or up to an hour in the oven at 180°C/350°F/Gas Mark 4.

Let it cool slightly, peel off the skin and then whizz the flesh in a food processor until it is a smooth purée.

Melt the chocolate in the microwave on a low setting for about 3 minutes. I put it in for a minute at a time and stir between each blast to make sure it doesn't burn. Or you can put the chocolate in a heat proof bowl on top of a pan filled with about 5cm /2-inches of barely simmering water. Make sure the bowl doesn't touch the water. Melt over a low heat, stirring occasionally.

Mix the melted chocolate with the aubergine purée.

Sweeten to taste with agave nectar or fruit sugar.

Thin the mixture with the cream and give everything a vigorous mix.

At this stage add raisins, chopped prunes or dairy free chocolate chips if you are using them.

Pour the mousse into some small dishes.

Top with some toasted chopped nuts or seeds (pumpkin, sunflower, or sesame) and refrigerate.

Take out of the fridge at least 20 minutes before you intend to eat it to get the best flavour.

BLOOD ORANGE ICED DESSERT

The sweet freshness of blood oranges cuts through the coconut in this to make a refreshing dessert. Canned coconut milk is much thicker and denser than drinking coconut milk, so is better for this dessert.

INGREDIENTS
SERVES 4

4 blood oranges

1 tbsp agave nectar

400ml/14 oz can coconut milk

METHOD

Cut the skin and pith off the oranges.

Cut between the membranes to remove the segments.

Place the segments on a tray and freeze until hard.

Blend half the frozen segments with the agave and coconut milk until smooth.

Add the rest of the orange and blend a little so there are chunks of orange left.

Pour into a lidded tub and freeze.

Remove from the freezer at least half an hour before you want to eat it.

COFFEE AND TIA MARIA ICE CREAM

We use shots of espresso coffee from our local coffee shop but if you have a home espresso machine you can make your own. I think the flavour of the hazelnut goes particularly well with a coffee liqueur but if you prefer you could also use almond or coconut milk.

Without the sugar the dessert has a quite adult taste which you may not find sweet enough for ice cream. The flavour matures in the freezer so try to make it a bit ahead of time.

INGREDIENTS
SERVES 6

600ml/1 ¼ pints/2 ½ cups hazelnut milk

6 shots (approx. 150ml/5fl oz/ $^2/_3$ cup) strong espresso coffee

150ml/5fl oz/ $^2/_3$ cup Tia Maria or other dairy-free coffee flavoured liqueur

1 heaped tbsp dark muscovado/raw sugar (optional)

85g/3 oz pecan nuts (optional)

METHOD

Mix together the hazelnut milk, coffee, liqueur and sugar, if you are using it, and put them into an ice cream maker.

Churn/freeze until it has reached 'slush' texture then add the pecan nuts if you are using them.

If you are serving the ice cream at once continue to churn/freeze until it is frozen but not frozen hard.

If you are not using it immediately continue to churn/freeze until it is frozen but remember to take it out of the freezer and soften in the microwave for two minutes on defrost or leave it in the fridge for at least 30 minutes before you want to eat it.

BANANA, COCONUT MILK AND GINGER ICE CREAM

This is a really tasty mixture, not, as so often can happen with banana, overwhelmed by the banana flavour. I am giving slightly more generous proportions as it seems a shame to make ice cream only for the one sitting. Canned coconut milk is much denser than the drinking variety so better for ice cream.

INGREDIENTS
SERVES 6

2 ripe bananas

1 x 400ml/14fl oz can coconut milk

juice of 2 lemons

4 pieces stem ginger, chopped small

2 tbsp flaked almonds (optional)

METHOD

In a food processor, purée the bananas with the coconut milk and lemon juice.

Depending on whether you want the stem ginger bitty or puréed into the mixture, purée it with the other ingredients or mix it in after they are puréed.

Stir in the flaked almonds if you are using them and freeze in an ice cream maker.

If you do not have an ice cream maker, freeze in the bowl, taking it out every 20 minutes or so to beat vigorously, until frozen.

Remove from the freezer to soften for at least 20 minutes before serving.

BAKING

||||||||||||||||||||||||||||

Chocolate oat crunchies

Katherine's raw cherry and walnut brownies

Lemon almond shortbread

Brown teff and ginger cookies

Mini dark choccy cookies

FREEE sponge layer cake

Apple and chestnut flour or polenta cake

Dark chocolate cake

Christmas cake

Royal icing/frosting

Marzipan

Ginger and banana loaf

Chive and potato scones

Coconut milk soda bread

Brown loaf with ground almonds

Making good vegan biscuits is not a problem; although they may be crumblier than if they had been made with butter, they retain all the flavour of a traditional non-vegan cookie or biscuit.

Eggless cakes, however, can be a bit more of an issue as, although there are many new vegan 'eggs' appearing on the market, none of them have yet achieved quite the combination of 'lift' and 'set' that you get with a real egg. Sponge cakes are particularly hard to get right, but I am happy to say that Clare Marriage, the co-founder of Dove's Farm, has hit the spot with her FREEE sponge layer cake.

Fruit cakes, especially rich fruit cakes, work particularly well eggless as you are looking for a much richer, heavier consistency. Fruit purées also work well as in the Apple and chestnut flour cake.

There are now so many good gluten-free everyday breads on the market that, rather than giving you an everyday loaf, I am giving you some interesting alternatives.

CHOCOLATE OAT CRUNCHIES

These are incredibly 'more-ish'...

INGREDIENTS
CUTS INTO 12 CRUNCHIES

200g/8 oz oats/oatmeal

50g/2 oz sultanas/golden raisins

100g/4 oz dairy-free dark chocolate broken into small pieces

50g/2 oz dairy-free spread

70g/3 oz rice, date, or other syrup — or black treacle/molasses

METHOD

Heat the oven to 180°C/350°F/Gas Mark 4.

Mix the oats/oatmeal, sultanas/golden raisins, and chocolate pieces.

Heat the spread with the syrup in a saucepan until both are melted, then add the oat mixture.

Stir well together then spread out in a baking/jelly roll tray — about 2 cm (¾-inch) thick.

Bake for 25–30 minutes or until they are lightly tanned.

Remove from the oven, cut into your chosen shapes, and leave to cool in the tin.

When cold, remove carefully with a spatula.

KATHERINE'S RAW CHERRY AND WALNUT BROWNIES

These are super rich and gooey — and super delicious.

INGREDIENTS
MAKES 16 SQUARES

100g/4 oz dates

100g/4 oz prunes

200g/8 oz cashew nuts

50g/2 oz cacao powder

100g/4 oz raisins

50g/2 oz walnuts

50g/2 oz dried cherries

extra cacao for dusting

METHOD

If your dates and prunes are on the dry side, soak them in some hot water for a little while to soften them up.

In a food processor, whizz the cashew nuts until they are relatively fine.

Add the cacao powder, raisins, dates and prunes and whizz until you have a dough.

Move the dough to a mixing bowl.

Roughly chop the walnuts and kneed into the mixture so they are spread evenly.

Lightly dust the cherries in cacao to stop them clumping and then kneed them into the mixture as before.

Line a 25 cm/10-inch square baking tin with baking parchment and dust the bottom with a small amount of cacao powder. Pour in the mixture.

Lightly dust the top with cacao powder to help reduce the stickiness of the surface then press the mixture into the tin as evenly as possible with your hands or with a spoon.

Place in the fridge to chill and then cut into 16 squares.

Store in an airtight container.

LEMON ALMOND SHORTBREAD

The biscuits/cookies are slightly crumblier than a normal shortbread — but taste excellent.

INGREDIENTS
MAKES APPROX. 12 BISCUITS/COOKIES

50g/2 oz dairy free spread or coconut oil

75g/3 oz light muscovado sugar

grated rind of 1 large lemon

100g/4 oz gluten-free plain flour mix

50g/2 oz ground almonds

METHOD

Heat the oven to 160°C/325°F/Gas Mark 3.

Beat the spread or coconut oil with the sugar and lemon rind with an electric whisk till soft and light.

Rub into the ground almonds and flour with your fingers, working as lightly as you can.

Spread the mixture out into the bottom of a tin or shape it into a round approximately 20 cm/8-inch across and bake for 15 minutes.

Remove from the oven and score diagonally with a sharp knife to make 12 diamond shaped biscuits. Return to the oven for another 5 minutes.

Cool slightly then cut along the score marks remove carefully, with a spatula, to a cooling rack/grid to get cold.

BROWN TEFF AND GINGER COOKIES

Teff flour is a delicious nutty brown flour made from the ancient grain, teff, which grows mainly in Ethiopia. It is naturally gluten free but also very high in protein, fibre, B vitamins and minerals. So not just very tasty but also very good for you.

INGREDIENTS
MAKES APPROX. 10 BISCUITS/COOKIES

50g/2 oz light muscovado/raw sugar

100g/4 oz brown teff flour

2 heaped tsp ground ginger

pinch salt

100g/4 oz dairy-free spread

METHOD

Heat the oven to 180°C/350°F/Gas mark 4.

Put all the dry ingredients in a food processor.

Add the spread in small pieces and process till breadcrumb-like.

Press the mixture into the bottom of a lightly oiled baking tray/sheet — about 1 cm/½-inch thick and bake for 30 minutes.

Remove from the oven and cut into biscuit/cookie shapes.

Return to the oven for a further 10 minutes.

Cool slightly in the tin then cut the biscuits out and remove carefully to a cooling rack/grid to cool completely.

MINI DARK CHOCCY COOKIES

These are very tasty little cookies, but you need to be careful not to burn them. Because they are so dark, it is easy to do!

INGREDIENTS
75g/3 oz dairy-free spread

75g/3 oz dark muscovado sugar or 50g/2 oz caster/superfine sugar

50g/2 oz rice flour

50g/2 oz gram/chickpea flour

50g/2 oz gluten/wheat-free cocoa powder

1 level tsp gluten/wheat-free baking powder/baking soda

METHOD

Heat the oven to 190°C/375°F/Gas Mark 5.

Beat the spread and sugar together till they are light and fluffy.

Sift together the flours, cocoa and baking powder/baking soda and beat them into the mixture.

Roll teaspoons of the mixture into balls with your hands then squash them flat and decorate with the back of a fork.

Transfer carefully onto a baking tray and bake for 10–15 minutes, taking care that they do not burn.

Remove the cookies from the oven, cool slightly then transfer them carefully (they are quite crumbly) onto a cooling rack/grid to cool completely.

FREEE SPONGE LAYER CAKE

Clare Marriage, co-founder of Doves Farm in the UK, who mill organic, ancient grain flours, spends much of her time experimenting and testing the recipes that appear on their FREEE gluten-free flour packs. She is especially pleased with this one, which she developed with their self-raising (self-rising) gluten-free flour. And so she should be as spurred on by the desire to be able to offer a really nice sponge cake to her teenage son's egg-allergic housemate, she has created a delicious egg-free and gluten-free sponge cake!

INGREDIENTS

1 tsp oil (for greasing)

½ a ripe banana

125g/5 oz sugar

6 tbsp sunflower oil

1 tbsp vanilla extract

150g/6 oz FREEE, self-raising (self-rising) flour

4 tbsp water

4 tbsp jam/jelly

1 tsp icing/confectioner's sugar

METHOD

Heat the oven to 190°C/375°F/Gas Mark 5.

Line an 18 cm/7-inch, round cake tin/pan with lightly oiled greaseproof/waxed paper.

Peel and mash the banana on a plate

Put the sugar, oil and vanilla into a large bowl and beat together until light and fluffy or do this in a food processor.

Add the flour and water and mix well. Beat the mashed banana into the mixture.

Tip the mixture into the prepared cake tin and smooth the top. Bake for 30-35 minutes.

Turn the sponge out onto a cooling rack/grid and leave to cool.

Using a bread knife, carefully slice the cold sponge in half horizontally.

Gently lift off the top half.

Spread the bottom half of the sponge with jam. Place the top half on top.

Sieve the icing sugar over the top of the cake.

APPLE AND CHESTNUT FLOUR OR POLENTA CAKE

The chestnut flour gives a delicious, sweet nuttiness to this cake which works really well with the sharpness of the apple. But if you can't or don't want to eat nuts, a coarse polenta also works well. Leaving the skin on the apples will add extra texture to the cake; if you would prefer it smoother, peel the apples.

INGREDIENTS

10 soft dates, stoned and chopped very small

2 large Bramley or sharp cooking apples — approx. 700g/1lb 5 oz of apple, cored and chopped small, skin on

250ml/9fl oz/1 cup water

125g/5 oz coconut oil or vegan spread

300g/12 oz chestnut flour or coarse polenta

4 heaped tsp gluten and wheat-free baking powder

pecan nuts, walnuts, or almonds to decorate (optional)

METHOD

If the dates are relatively dry, cover with boiling water and soak for 15 minutes. Strain the dates but keep the soaking water to use as part of the water below.

Heat the oven to 180°C/350°F/Gas Mark 4.

Put the chopped apple with the chopped dates in a pan with the water. Bring to the boil, cover, and cook gently for 10–15 minutes or until the apple is totally soft.

In a bowl beat the coconut oil or spread with a wooden spoon until soft.

Gradually beat in the apple purée, then thoroughly fold in the chestnut flour or polenta along with the baking powder.

Line the base of a 20 cm/8-inch cake tin with greaseproof paper and spoon in the mixture.

Tap the tin on your worksurface until the cake mixture levels out then decorate with the nuts if you are using them.

Bake for 50 minutes or until a skewer comes out clean.

Cool slightly in the tin then turn out and allow to cool completely on a cooling rack/grid.

DARK CHOCOLATE CAKE

This recipe makes quite a small, but rich cake. To make a larger cake, just double the ingredients and cook for an extra 15 minutes, or until a skewer comes out clean.

INGREDIENTS

150g/6 oz dairy-free/vegan spread

150g/6 oz pale muscovado/raw sugar

3 tbsp gluten-free cocoa powder

3 tbsp boiling water

150g/6 oz flour gluten free self-raising/self-rising flour mix

4 tsp gluten and wheat-free baking powder/baking soda

50ml/2fl oz/¼ cup vegan milk – nut, oat, soya, or coconut

100g/4 oz undyed glacé cherries or chopped dried apricots (optional)

METHOD

Heat the oven to 180°C/350°F/Gas Mark 4.

Beat the spread and sugar in an electric mixer until light and fluffy.

Mix the cocoa powder with the boiling water to a smooth paste, then beat into the spread mixture.

Sieve the flour with the baking powder/baking soda and fold into the mixture with the milk and the cherries if you are using them.

Turn into a lined and greased 15 cm/6-inch cake tin/pan and bake for 45 minutes.

Remove from the oven and cool on a cooling rack/grid before cutting.

CHRISTMAS CAKE

This is a serious Christmas cake with lots of fruit — it will make a 20 cm/8-inch cake. However, because it is egg free, it will not keep as well as an eggy cake so try to make it only a day or two before it is to be eaten. And unless you have a large Christmas gathering you might want to halve the quantities of ingredients to make a smaller 15 cm/6-inch cake in which case reduce the baking time to 45-50 minutes but, as always, test with a skewer.

If you don't want to eat oats, you can substitute them with 100g/4 oz of buckwheat or teff flour, to give that slightly darker, nuttier taste and texture — or just go with 350g/14 oz, self-raising/self-rising flour.

INGREDIENTS
100g/4 oz soft dried apricots

100g/4 oz coconut oil or vegan spread

100g/4 oz agave syrup or dark muscovado/raw sugar

1 large Bramley cooking apple or 2 sharp eating apples, peeled and cored

200g/8 oz raisins

100g/4 oz sultanas/golden raisins

100g/4 oz currants

3 pieces stem ginger, chopped (optional)

250g/10 oz self-raising/self-rising gluten-free flour

2 level tsp each ground cinnamon and nutmeg

4 heaped tsp gluten and wheat-free baking powder

100g/4 oz gluten-free rolled oats

approx. 200ml/7fl oz/ 2/3 cup apple juice, orange juice or brandy or a mixture of juice and brandy

METHOD

If the apricots are very dry soak them in boiling water for 5–10 minutes depending on how dry they are.

Heat the oven to 180°C/350°F/Gas Mark 4.

Meanwhile, beat the coconut oil or dairy-free spread with the agave syrup or muscovado sugar until creamy.

Drain the apricots and then purée them with the apple in a food processor. Add the sugar and spread and whizz again briefly. Transfer to a bowl.

Add the raisins, sultanas/golden raisins, currants, and ginger if you are using it and mix well.

Sieve together the flour, spices and baking powder then fold into the mixture along with the oats and the liquid. You want the mixture to be wet but not sloppy. Make sure it is well mixed.

Line a 20 cm/8-inch cake tin with oiled greaseproof paper, spoon in the mixture. Tap the cake tin on your worksurface to level out the top of the tin, then bake for approximately 1 hr 20 minutes, or until a skewer comes out clean.

Cool for 15 minutes in the tin then turn out onto a cooling rack/grid, peel off the greaseproof paper and allow to cool completely before icing, if you are going to do so.

ROYAL ICING/FROSTING

INGREDIENTS
TO COVER 20 CM/8-INCH CAKE

350g/14 oz vegetable shortening — Trex or Crisco

approx. 600g/1 lb 6 oz icing/confectioner's sugar

vanilla or almond essence to taste

METHOD
Beat the shortening with the sugar in a food mixer until well mixed, smooth, and creamy. You might find it easier to do the last bit of mixing with your hand.

Add vanilla or almond essence (a few drops at a time as they are quite strong) and more sugar if you think you need it and beat again.

Cover with cling film and store in the fridge or a cool larder until needed. It will keep almost indefinitely.

MARZIPAN

INGREDIENTS

400g/14 oz ground almonds

180-200g/7-8 oz icing/confectioner's sugar

8 tbsp vegetable shortening – Trex or Crisco

almond essence to taste

METHOD

Mix the ground almonds thoroughly with the sugar.

Work the shortening with your hand until it is very soft then work in the dry ingredients.

Add extra flavour with almond essence, a few drops at a time as it is quite strong, and a little more sugar if it is not sweet enough.

Wrap in cling film and store in the fridge or a cool larder until needed. It will keep almost indefinitely.

TO ICE THE CAKE

EXTRA INGREDIENTS
Apricot jam/jelly

Warm a tablespoon of jam/jelly in a saucepan.

Spread a very thin layer of jam/jelly over the top and down the sides of the cake.

Lay a piece of cling film out on a board and sprinkle over some icing/confectioner's sugar.

Gently roll out the marzipan then, with the help of the cling film roll it over the rolling pin and then onto the cake. Don't worry if it breaks as you can stick it together with your fingers and it will all be covered by the frosting!

Pat it down all round the cake making sure that there are no gaps and that it is fairly smooth.

With a wide-bladed knife or spatula, spread the icing/frosting over the marzipan. You can make it rough and snow-like or smooth it out (using your spatula dipped in hot water) as you prefer.

Make sure that all the marzipan is covered.

Decorate as you fancy!

GINGER AND BANANA LOAF

The texture of this loaf is cakey rather than bready — but it does not quite qualify as a cake! However, it is delicious — and it is gingery... If you like gentle rather than vigorous ginger flavouring, reduce the amount of stem ginger to 40g/1½ oz.

INGREDIENTS
2 medium sized ripe bananas

50g/2 oz vegan spread

1–3 tbsp agave, maple, or golden syrup, depending on how sweet you want your loaf

40–60g/1½ – 2 oz piece of stem ginger in its syrup, depending on how gingery you want your loaf

100g/4 oz buckwheat flour

50g/2 oz brown rice flour

2 heaped tsp gluten and wheat-free baking powder/baking soda

1 heaped tsp powdered ginger

2 large tbsp plain coconut or soya yogurt

METHOD

Heat the oven to 180°C/350°F/Gas mark 4.

Mash the bananas with the butter or spread, in a food processor — or mash the bananas with a fork and then beat with the fat in a mixer.

Beat in whichever syrup you are using.

Cut the stem ginger into small pieces and add to the mixture.

Sieve the buckwheat and rice flour with the baking powder/baking soda and the ginger and fold half into the banana mixture alternatively with the yogurt.

Line a 20 cm/8-inch loaf tin with greaseproof/waxed paper and oil lightly.

Spoon in the mixture, smooth the top. Bake for 30–35 minutes or until a skewer comes out clean.

Allow to cool slightly in the tin before turning out and to finish cooling on a cooling rack/grid.

CHIVE AND POTATO SCONES

A great, old-fashioned, Irish country recipe.

MAKES 8 SCONES

INGREDIENTS

450g/1 lb floury potatoes, peeled and cut into chunks

130g/4½ oz plain/all-purpose gluten/wheat-free flour, sifted

3 tbsp olive oil

2 tbsp snipped chives

vegetable oil for greasing

salt and ground black pepper

METHOD

Cook the potatoes in a saucepan of boiling salted water for 15 minutes or until tender and then drain thoroughly.

Put potatoes in a clean pan and mash them.

Add the flour, olive oil and chives with a little salt and pepper and mix to a soft dough.

Roll out on a floured board to a thickness of 5 mm/¼-inch.

Cut into rounds with a 5 cm/2-inch pastry cutter.

Lightly grease, then heat a griddle or frying pan and place the scones on it.

Cook over a low heat, in batches if necessary, for approximately 10 minutes, turning once, until the scones are golden brown on both sides.

COCONUT MILK SODA BREAD

This mixture makes a really tasty, coarse brown soda bread – quite solid but a great flavour.

INGREDIENTS
100g/4 oz buckwheat flour

150g/6 oz gram/chickpea flour

50g/2 oz millet flakes

50g/2 oz potato flour

1 level tsp salt

2 level tsp bicarbonate of soda

2 level tsp cream of tartar

1 heaped tsp xanthan gum

300ml/10fl oz coconut milk

juice ½ lemon

METHOD

Heat the oven to 190°C/375°F/Gas Mark 5.

Flour a baking tray.

Mix all the dry ingredients well together.

Form a well in the centre and add the coconut milk and lemon juice.

Incorporate it quickly and lightly into the dough which will be quite wet.

Form the dough into a round loaf shape and cut a cross on the top with a wet knife.

Bake for 40 minutes then remove from the oven, ease gently off the tray with a spatula and cool on a cooling rack/grid.

BROWN LOAF WITH GROUND ALMONDS

This loaf needs time to rise, so don't rush it! It has a very slight and rather pleasantly sweet aftertaste thanks to the dark muscovado sugar and the almonds, which also help to keep it moist.

MAKES 1 LARGE LOAF

INGREDIENTS

100g/4 oz buckwheat flour

100g/4 oz gram/chickpea flour

100g/4 oz rice flour

50g/2 oz ground almonds

1 tsp sea salt

2 heaped tsp dark muscovado sugar

1 scant tsp xanthan gum

1 x 7g/¼ oz sachet easy baker's yeast

3 tbsp olive oil

400ml /14fl oz/1 2/3 cups lukewarm water

METHOD

Mix the flours, almonds salt, sugar, xanthan gum and yeast in the bowl of a mixer then beat in the olive oil and warm water.

Continue to beat till you have a smooth dough.

Turn the dough into a well-greased loaf tin, smooth the top with a wet spoon, cover with cling film and prove for 30-45 minutes in an airing cupboard or a warming oven.

Heat the oven to 200°C/400°F/Gas Mark 6.

Remove the clingfilm and bake for 45 minutes or until the bread sounds hollow when rapped. Turn out onto a cooling rack/grid to cool.

53599696R00139